PUT YOURSELF IN THEIR PLACE 3
Part I

Bible characters from the Acts, dramatically portrayed
for study, discussion and meditation

by Jane Archer

with illustrations by Brian Evans

For my husband John

CONTENTS

INTRODUCTION

Make me a captive, Lord,
And then I shall be free

As I delved into the life of the Early Church and attempted to eavesdrop on the confidences of its 'big names', these words from George Matheson's hymn flashed up on my mental computer screen. They seemed so appropriate to Peter, Paul and the others that I fetched my hymn-book to check how the verse continued:

Force me to render up my sword, and I shall conqueror be.
I sink in life's alarms when by myself I stand;
Imprison me within thine arms, and strong shall be my hand.

I'm sure that would have made a great deal of sense to Paul, who had been so ready with his fists until God took him in hand; real power only came to him when he swapped aggression and violence for ways of peace and love. As with my previous research into characters from scripture, I was struck by the timelessness of human nature. The words of that hymn were written in the late nineteenth century, but they are just as applicable to the Christians of the first century AD, and to us embarking on the twenty-first century. It is this consistency of human nature which enables us to be helped by a study of the Bible personalities, since many of their experiences are essentially the same as ours. Despite the passage of two thousand years with its cavalcade of cultures and lifestyles, these people experienced hope and fear, excitement and disappointment, ambition and apathy, love and hate – just as we do. So perhaps we can glean some tips from them for our Christian journey.

The second verse of that hymn advises:

My power is faint and low till I have learned to serve;
It wants the needed fire to glow, it wants the breeze to nerve.

This encapsulates the message of the Acts: it is through the fire or the wind of God's Holy Spirit that we 'glow' and are 'nerved' for service. Can this fire which drove the early Christians to such feats of faith and courage inject new life and energy into the often lacklustre witness of twenty-first century Christians?

This third book in the series is in two parts. The twenty-eight chapters of Acts contain too many significant personalities for one book, and so I have divided them into two groups. Peter and nine others associated with the Early Church in Jerusalem comprise the ten chapters of Part I; Paul and some people featured in his journeys form the substance of Part II. As in my previous books, each chapter begins with a dramatic speech or dialogue designed to bring the character to life. Needless to say, the words are imaginary, but each individual is carefully researched to discover as much as possible from the available evidence about these men and women from the past. Each portrait is further illustrated with a line drawing, the interpretation of which may itself prompt discussion. I hope that, by listening to the words and studying the material provided, the members of your group will not only learn more about themselves and each other, but will absorb something of the exuberance, vitality and comfort of the Holy Spirit which so empowered the early Christians in the service of their Saviour.

Practical tips for the use of the book

1. It is primarily intended for group use and is suitable for a wide range of ages, but, if preferred, it can serve as a focus for private study and meditation. The character dialogues might be useful bases for dramatic presentations in schools or in church services around Pentecost.

2. To achieve the greatest impact, the character dialogues should be acted, or read aloud following a little preparation. If the group member can be prevailed upon to dress up appropriately, so much the better! The use of local accents will add more colour and credibility to some, e.g. Dorcas would probably sound quite 'posh', whereas Captain Cornelius might have some sort of regional accent.

3. The device of anachronism is used at times, with the intention of drawing the character closer to our experience: Matthias exclaims: 'It would have made your biggest blockbuster movie look like a bedtime story!' This has a contemporary ring which may help to add flesh and blood to the character.

4. The dramatic passages are followed by Bible extracts and references relating to the character. The Bible extracts printed in full give scriptural backing for much of the material in the dramatic script, and the leader is advised to use this with the group as they consider the character. This should prevent preoccupation with details which are purely imaginary and less relevant to serious discussion. The other Bible references may help to paint a wider background to the issues raised.

5. Following the Bible references, there are lists of discussion topics, each list being fairly long to allow a leader to make a selection appropriate to his group. Straightforward questions are included, together with others of a more searching nature to encourage growth of group fellowship through shared experience.

6. Each chapter ends with a prayer focusing on a theme from the material; some have been specially composed, others have been drawn from our Christian heritage.

7. It is important that members of the group understand clearly the imaginative nature of each dialogue. People should feel free to question the interpretations and make their own suggestions.

8. A bibliography at the end of the book offers some guidance on sources of background information.

MATTHIAS

Better late than never! Those words were written for me, I guess! For years I desperately wanted to be one of the chosen twelve who went with Jesus of Nazareth, and now that he has left us . . . only now . . . I get voted on to the group! Poor old Matt! And yet, what an honour! I still can't believe it, and that's after nearly two weeks. Just think . . . a stone falls and hey presto! my whole life changes. If only it could have happened three years ago, but that's life!

My goodness, your faces are completely blank, and no wonder! You don't know **what** I'm talking about, do you? The trouble is things have moved so quickly these last few weeks, and such earth-shattering events have taken place – you tend to assume everyone's heard it all. But let me fill you in. The atmosphere in Jerusalem right now is positively **electric**, and that's what I've got to get over to you.

My name is Matthias and I'm a very ordinary sort . . . certainly not someone you'd notice in the street. There's no one waiting to write my biography . . . for the very good reason that I've never done anything worth writing about! So I don't need to bore you with my CV – as you would call it. But the memorable bit began about two weeks ago, when I seemed to be catapulted into the limelight.

What you certainly will know is the terrible tragedy that happened to our beloved friend, Jesus – how he was crucified by the authorities although he had never harmed a soul. And then his fantastic rising again from the tomb – you're bound to have heard all about that? Talk about an emotional roller-coaster! One minute we were plunged in despair, the next wildly elated by his presence back with us. But now he's gone again, and that's how it's going to stay. He explained it to us all, here in Jerusalem. What he actually said was we couldn't know the future, but the Holy Spirit would be coming soon to fill us with power, so that we could be witnesses for him all over the world. Then he just sort of vanished away.

Sure enough, about ten days later – Pentecost time, it was – the Holy Spirit certainly did come, with a vengeance, if you'll pardon the expression! It would have made your biggest blockbuster movie look like a bedtime story! We were all chatting quietly together when suddenly this huge draught started to blow everything about with a great roaring noise – like a mini-hurricane. Then flames popped up everywhere and yet nothing was burning! They licked round us all – you'd have sworn they touched each person individually, yet nobody was hurt. But what happened was we were all **galvanised** – that's the best word I can think of – absolutely uplifted with a feeling of power. People started clamouring in all sorts of languages and yet you could understand everything they said. Well, we just didn't know what had hit us. Then Peter got up and explained to everyone that this was the Holy Spirit, but, of course, most people were completely bowled over and didn't know what to do next. Peter urged them to repent and be baptised in the name of Jesus, and, do you know, about three thousand people did just that! Unbelievable! In fact even as I describe it all, it sounds like huge exaggeration, but I'm not one for flights of fancy – what I've told you is the plain and simple truth, I swear it.

Mind you, I've wandered completely from the point – distracted again by all this excitement. I started to tell you how I was voted on to the group of apostles, didn't I? Anyway . . . what happened was the group needed a replacement, because they had been one short ever since Judas Iscariot turned traitor. They had to make the number up to twelve again, like the tribes of Israel, in order to bear out what it says in the Psalms. So how do you choose? Peter told them it was essential the new man had been around with Jesus and the group right from the start, and had witnessed his resurrection and all the get-togethers after that until he left us. A number of us fitted the bill, but they only nominated two – me and Joseph Barsabbas. Prayers were said and then they drew lots. As you've guessed, I was the lucky one. I feel quite sorry for Joseph.

Since that moment, believe me, things have **not stopped!** Fitting in with the apostles' way of life isn't a problem, because I've been around with them for years now, despite not being one of the Twelve. I've been used to all the sharing of possessions, dishing out of cash – that sort of thing. But it's the responsibility now – the urgency of it! It's like a fire raging inside me, driving me to work and witness for Jesus every hour of the day. I pray that I'll prove worthy of their choice. It's the most important thing that's ever happened in my life, and I intend to give it all I've got!

BIBLE PASSAGES

Acts 1:15-26

A few days later there was a meeting of the believers, about 120 in all, and Peter stood up to speak. 'My fellow-believers,' he said, 'the scripture had to come true in which the Holy Spirit, speaking through David, made a prediction about Judas, who was the guide for those who arrested Jesus. Judas was a member of our group, for he had been chosen to have a part in our work.'

6

(With the money that Judas got for his evil act he bought a field, where he fell to his death; he burst open and all his bowels spilt out. All the people living in Jerusalem heard about it, and so in their own language they call that field Akeldama, which means 'Field of Blood'.)

For it is written in the book of Psalms:
> 'May his house become empty;
>   may no one live in it.'

It is also written:
>   'May someone else take his place of service.'

So then, someone must join us as a witness to the resurrection of the Lord Jesus. He must be one of the men who were in our group during the whole time that the Lord Jesus travelled about with us, beginning from the time John preached his message of baptism until the day Jesus was taken up from us to heaven.'

So they proposed two men: Joseph, who was called Barsabbas (also known as Justus), and Matthias. Then they prayed, 'Lord, you know the thoughts of everyone, so show us which of these two you have chosen to serve as an apostle in the place of Judas, who left to go to the place where he belongs.' Then they drew lots to choose between the two men, and the one chosen was Matthias, who was added to the group of eleven apostles.

Acts 2:1-12

When the day of Pentecost came, all the believers were gathered together in one place. Suddenly there was a noise from the sky which sounded like a strong wind blowing, and it filled the whole house where they were sitting. Then they saw what looked like tongues of fire which spread out and touched each person there. They were all filled with the Holy Spirit and began to talk in other languages, as the Spirit enabled them to speak.

There were Jews living in Jerusalem, religious people who had come from every country in the world. When they heard this noise, a large crowd gathered. They were all excited, because each one of them heard the believers speaking in his or her own language. In amazement and wonder they exclaimed, 'These people who are talking like this are Galileans! How is it, then, that all of us hear them speaking in our own native languages? We are from Parthia, Media, and Elam; from Mesopotamia, Judea, and Cappadocia; from Pontus and Asia, from Phrygia and Pamphylia, from Egypt and the regions of Libya near Cyrene. Some of us are from Rome, both Jews and

Gentiles converted to Judaism, and some of us are from Crete and Arabia – yet all of us hear them speaking in our own languages about the great things that God has done!' Amazed and confused, they kept asking each other, 'What does this mean?'

ADDITIONAL BIBLE REFERENCES FOR PRIVATE STUDY

Acts 1:3-9

Acts 2:14-42

BACKGROUND NOTES

1. Author of Acts

Reference is made in Matthias' speech to the Ascension of Jesus. Luke was the writer of Acts, and he had concluded his Gospel with a description of that event *(Luke 24:50-53)*. Acts, which was probably written towards the end of the first century AD, and which can be considered a continuation of Luke's record of the activities of Jesus and his followers, begins from that traumatic event. It describes the coming of the Holy Spirit and the spread of the Christian faith from Jerusalem to Rome, the heart of the Empire, and it contains a succession of dramas, many of them prompted by the working of the Holy Spirit.

2. The Holy Spirit

The Acts could easily have been sub-titled 'The Diary of the Holy Spirit', and so one paragraph of study notes about such an essential ingredient of the Christian faith is, of course, woefully inadequate. Nevertheless this book would be incomplete without it.

We tend to think that the Holy Spirit came into being at Pentecost, but this is not the case. He is – and always has been – a third part of the essence of God, who is Father, Son and Holy Spirit. In Acts 1:16 Peter mentions the Holy Spirit speaking through David, although the day of Pentecost has not yet happened. What is clear is that something very special did happen on that day, and the Holy Spirit became a conspicuous and powerful force in the lives of the believers. From that dramatic moment in the Upper Room, the Holy Spirit guided them, became a source of courage, power, inspiration and joy to them, and filled their whole being so unmistakably that all who came into contact with them, recognised his presence. Moreover, to the twelve apostles, the

Holy Spirit was given in such a way at Pentecost that he could be conveyed to others through the laying-on of hands.

William Barclay notes that in the first thirteen chapters of Acts there are more than forty references to the Holy Spirit, a clear indication that *the early church was a Spirit-filled church and that was the source of its power'*.

3. Casting of lots

Lotteries are very much part of our contemporary scene, particularly since the launch of the much-debated National Lottery in 1994. It is interesting to note, however, that this method of selection features as far back as the earliest events recorded in the Bible. When the Israelites conquered Canaan, the Lord told Moses that the land should be divided by lot *(Joshua 14:2)*. The practice of casting lots was common throughout Israel and the ancient world, and involved placing stones of particular colours or markings into a container which was shaken until one jumped out. This was the chosen one. The practice was thought to preclude any possibility of human choice since it placed the issue firmly in God's hands. Equally there could be no fear of influence through magic or witchcraft, because people were convinced the decision was entirely the Lord's. *'Men cast lots to learn God's will, but God himself determines the answer' (Proverbs 16:33)*.

Thus, in the case of Matthias, we must understand not that the Eleven selected Matthias, but that Jesus was choosing him just as he had previously chosen the others.

In Britain over the centuries we have nurtured a love-hate relationship with lotteries. In 1566 Queen Elizabeth I established the first English national lottery in order to raise money for harbour repairs. The practice then continued until 1826, when corruption by lottery organisers caused it to be banned. No further national lottery was permitted until the present one.

4. Psalms

Peter referred to the Psalms in order to show the people how Judas had acted in accordance with the divine purpose laid down in the scriptures. They were to see it as part of the Passion which providence necessitated should happen to the Messiah. The psalm to which Matthias alludes in his script is Psalm 109:8:

May his life soon be ended;
May another man take his job!

DISCUSSION TOPICS

1. Do you believe in luck? Is there such a thing?

2. What do you think about the sending of Good Luck cards?

3. Is your church 'galvanised' by the Holy Spirit? Can you think of particular times or occasions when it has been?

4. What are your feelings about the coming of the Holy Spirit to the disciples in the Upper Room? Can you relate to it or does it seem very strange?

5. What lessons can we learn from the way of life of the apostles and followers of the Early Church? What practices do we have in common?

6. The believers shared everything together. As Christians in the twenty-first century, should we view the concept of sharing in the same way? If not, how important should we rate it, and what practice should we follow?

7. What is the most important thing in your life? How much time/energy do you devote to it?

An Apostle had to bear witness to / fact that J. was alive. This equally applies to / Xtian today. How does J. come alive for me?

PRAYER

Come, Holy Ghost, our souls inspire,
And lighten with celestial fire;
Thou the anointing Spirit art,
Who dost thy sevenfold gifts impart:

Thy blessèd unction from above
Is comfort, life, and fire of love;
Enable with perpetual light
The dullness of our blinded sight:

Anoint and cheer our soilèd face
With the abundance of thy grace;
Keep far our foes, give peace at home;
Where thou art guide no ill can come.

Teach us to know the Father, Son,
And thee, of both, to be but One;
That through the ages all along
This may be our endless song:

'Praise to thy eternal merit,
Father, Son, and Holy Spirit. Amen.'

9th Century –
translated by John Cosin (1594-1672)

LAME MAN AT THE BEAUTIFUL GATE

What d'you think of that gate, friends? Isn't it amazing? Bronze, that is . . . from Corinth, they say. Must have cost an arm and a leg. But that King Herod never was short of a penny or two where his pretty buildings were concerned. Isn't it beautiful? Well, course it is – that's why they call it the Beautiful Gate! And I'm telling you, it can look even better than that. If you were here when the sun was up at its highest, you'd be having to turn your eyes away . . . completely blinds you, that bronze, when it catches the light.

But you're probably thinking 'Come on, mate! This is a bit over the top! A gate's a gate, when all's said and done!' That's as may be, but suppose I tell you that, until a few weeks ago, I spent all my waking hours – day in day out – for forty long years, beside that gate. It was my home, if you like. Puts a different perspective on it, maybe? But then you'll reason I must have been making a quick buck at the stalls over there, flogging pigeons for sacrifice or something. Is that it? Well, you'd be wrong, see! I was there, friends . . . sitting in a miserable huddle . . . because there was nothing else on this earth that I was fit for! And that's the honest truth. What used to happen was my mates would carry me here every morning at first light, so I was ready with my begging bowl when folks came past for prayer. And the reason they did that was because my legs had opted out the day I was born – absolutely useless they were – and if you don't believe me, ask anyone around.

But don't think I'm looking for sympathy – far from it! Listen to this! If you found the cripple bit hard to take, this'll really stretch you!

On this particular afternoon I was sitting here same as usual when these followers of Jesus of Nazareth turned up. Nothing odd about that – they often came by at three o'clock on their way to prayers at the Temple. I'd seen them lots. And of course I'd heard all the low-down on their activities around the place. But there was nothing to make me think this day would turn out different from any other. I held my bowl up automatically as they came near, and muttered my usual 'Spare a penny, kind sirs!' or something like that, and then it all happened! The big guy, Peter, stopped dead in his tracks, and fixed me with such a stare it rattled me. Couldn't make out whether he was going to give me money or lay into me. His mate, John, was staring too. Then Peter says really sharply, 'Look right at us!' Fair put the wind up me! Thoughts flash through my head like 'I can't get away, no-one to help, I'm finished if he arrests me' – blind panic! But it wasn't that at all. His next words were 'I haven't any money; but what I do have I'm giving to you', and as I'm trying to fathom that one out, he shouts, 'In the name of Jesus Christ of Nazareth, I order you to get up and walk!' Then he grabs my right hand and heaves me up on to my useless feet! What power! He's a giant! But just as I thought my feet would sag as they usually did, this strength came surging through them and up my legs, and – believe it or not – I stayed upright! Steady and straight, I was, just like you!

I was speechless! Don't know how long I stood there, then I remember walking round in circles, testing my feet to see if they would hold. Must have looked gaga! When the penny dropped that Peter had cured me – sorry! **his God** had cured me . . . through the name of Jesus, he explained – I just went crazy! I jumped around and whooped and shouted, 'Praises to God! Praises to God!' and acted like a complete freak. The two guys went into the Temple so I charged after them. I remember grabbing hold of one and hanging on like a limpet – I guess I was scared if I lost them it would all return to normal. What a day! Imagine the crowds! Dumbfounded, they were, all surging round asking what on earth had happened. Of course Peter seized the opportunity and started telling everyone about Jesus and how we were to blame for letting him get killed. We couldn't help it, he said, we were just ignorant. Anyway, God had brought Jesus back to life, and it was through the power of his name that I had been cured. He said everyone could be helped if they turned to God and repented. Marvellous, isn't it? I'll certainly be sticking with this from now on. I want to know more about this fantastic Jesus.

The awful bit was that Peter and John got arrested for this. Can you believe it? Jealousy, I reckon! They were put on trial by the Sanhedrin, but of course they got off – would have been a riot otherwise. But walls have ears! I'd better watch what I say, or I might be next.

So that's it! See now why this gate's a bit special for me? It's like the gate to my new life.

BIBLE PASSAGES

Acts 3:1-10

One day Peter and John went to the Temple at three o'clock in the afternoon, the hour for prayer. There at the Beautiful Gate, as it was called, was a man who had been lame all his life. Every day he was carried to the gate to beg for money from the people who were going into the Temple. When he saw Peter and John going in, he begged them to give him something. They looked straight at him, and Peter said, 'Look at us!' So he looked at them, expecting to get something from them. But Peter said to him, 'I have no money at all, but I give you what I have: in the name of Jesus Christ of Nazareth I order you to get up and walk!' Then he took him by his right hand and helped him up. At once the man's feet and ankles became strong; he jumped up, stood on his feet, and started walking around. Then he went into the Temple with them, walking and jumping and praising God. The people there saw him walking and praising God, and when they recognised him as the beggar who had sat at the Beautiful Gate, they were all surprised and amazed at what had happened to him.

Acts 4:5-17

The next day the Jewish leaders, the elders, and the teachers of the Law gathered in Jerusalem. They met with the High Priest Annas and with Caiaphas, John, Alexander, and the others who belonged to the High Priest's family. They made the apostles stand before them and asked them, 'How did you do this? What power have you got or whose name did you use?'

Peter, full of the Holy Spirit, answered them, 'Leaders of the people and elders: if we are being questioned today about the good deed done to the lame man and how he was healed, then you should all know, and all the people of Israel should know, that this man stands here before you completely well through the power of the name of Jesus Christ of Nazareth – whom you crucified and whom God raised from death. Jesus is the one of whom the scripture says:

'The stone that you the builders despised
turned out to be the most important of all.'

Salvation is to be found through him alone; in all the world there is no one else whom God has given who can save us.'

The members of the Council were amazed to see how bold Peter and John were and to learn that they were ordinary men of no education. They realised then that they had been companions of Jesus. But there was nothing that they could say, because they saw the man who had been healed, standing there with Peter and John. So they told them to leave the Council room, and then they started discussing among themselves. 'What shall we do with these men?' they asked. 'Everyone in Jerusalem knows that this extraordinary miracle has been performed by them, and we cannot deny it. But to keep this matter from spreading any further among the people, let us warn these men never again to speak to anyone in the name of Jesus.'

Isaiah 35:6

> The lame will leap and dance,
> And those who cannot speak will shout for joy.
> Streams of water will flow through the desert.

ADDITIONAL BIBLE REFERENCES FOR PRIVATE STUDY

Acts 3:11-26

Acts 4:1-4

Matthew 28:16-20

BACKGROUND NOTES

1. Herod the Great

Herod was King of the Jews from 37-4BC. His reign was marked by an extensive programme of building, and vast numbers of local labourers, Roman engineers and Greek architects were all employed in his lavish schemes. His desert fortress, Herodium, involved flattening the top of a hill to provide a huge platform for his giant structure, said by one writer to resemble a fortress emerging from a volcano! The city of Jerusalem was transformed into an architectural showpiece, with numerous grandiose palaces, splendid public buildings, handsome walls, an ornate Greek-style theatre etc. In 20BC Herod embarked on his *pièce de résistance* – an ambitious rebuilding of the Temple. It would surpass even the magnificence of Solomon's Temple, but the work was to continue long after Herod's death.

2. The Beautiful Gate

Scholars have not been able to identify this gate conclusively, but most now favour the Nicanor Gate, which formed the main eastern entrance to the Temple precincts through the Court of the Women. This description is found in *The Jewish War* by the first century historian, Josephus, with his eye for detail:

On the north and south the gates numbered eight, four in each case; on the east there were bound to be two, for on this side a special place was walled off for the women to worship in, necessitating a second gate, which opened facing the first. On the other sides there was one north and one south gate through which the Court of the Women could be entered; for women were neither admitted through the others nor allowed to go past the dividing wall via their own gate. This court was open for worship alike to native women and to Jewesses from abroad. The western part had no gate at all, there being no openings in the wall on that side. The colonnades between the gates faced inwards from the wall in front of the treasury, and rested on pillars of exceptional height and beauty; they were single, but apart from size were in every way equal to those round the lower court.

Of the gates nine were completely covered with gold and silver . . . but the one outside the Sanctuary was of Corinthian bronze, and far more valuable than those overlaid with silver or even gold . . . The other gates were all of the same size, but the one beyond the Corinthian Gate, opening out from the Court of the Women on the east and facing the gate of the Sanctuary, was much bigger; for its height was 75 feet, that of the doors 50, and the decoration was more magnificent.

3. Temple Prayers

It is interesting to note that by observing prayer time at the Temple, Peter and John were still continuing the Jewish practice to which they were accustomed. They clearly saw no problem marrying the old tradition with their new way of life.

In Judaism the day began at 6am and ended at 6pm, and there were three special hours of prayer: at 9am, 12 noon and 3pm. The last corresponded with the hour of evening sacrifice. Devout Jews believed that all prayer to God was effective, but it was particularly powerful when offered at the Temple.

It was customary for beggars to position themselves at the entrance to a temple on the assumption that worshippers would be in the right frame of mind to offer charity. For their part, the worshippers would earn merit for their compassion.

DISCUSSION TOPICS

1. Have you any experience of apparently miraculous healing?

2. Do you think healing services should be part of the life of every church?

3. Do you find your Christian faith helpful when you are supporting people who are sick?

4. Does more need to be done to help people with disabilities in
     a) your church?
     b) your community?

5. Would visitors see your church as a group of people who praise God enthusiastically? What do you think would strike them most about the worship and activities of your church?

6. How would you explain what it means to follow Jesus?

PRAYER

Father, we thank you for the gifts of health and strength:
For the feeling of well-being when we awake to the new day;
For senses which enable us to marvel at the sights, sounds and scents of creation;
For energy which drives us to work at tasks and enterprises;
For warm hearts and searching minds;
For relaxation which brings us peaceful sleep.
Teach us to value these everyday blessings, and use them to the full in your service.

We pray for people in every land whose lives are restricted by illness or disability, especially those who have suffered a long time.
Surround them with your love, and keep the light of hope in their eyes;
Calm their fears, and help them to put their trust in you;
Reassure them that you will always be with them, even in the darkest hours.

Bless those whose lives are dedicated to the care and healing of the sick. Give them wisdom, skill and understanding, and may they rejoice in the knowledge that they are following the example of Jesus Christ our healing Saviour. Help us all to recognise our duty to ease the burdens of the suffering in whatever way we are able.

AMEN

GAMALIEL

'Storms come, and the wicked are blown away, but honest people are always safe.' That's it! Why didn't I think of it? It illustrates the point perfectly, but it has only just come to me . . . I must be going rusty in my old age! I love the old proverbs – such obvious everyday statements on the surface, but with pearls of wisdom tucked inside!

Ah! My goodness me! I have visitors! I do beg your pardon. You have stumbled on the ramblings of a forgetful old bookworm! Let me introduce myself and make amends. My name is Gamaliel. I am a member of the Sanhedrin, a Pharisee, a Doctor of Law and a teacher. There! Now you have it! And I suppose, to complete the picture, you should know that I am the grandson of the Rabbi Hillel, a greatly respected teacher renowned for his tolerance and moderation. If **I** am honoured just a little for the wisdom of my teaching – then **he** was universally revered as the veritable King Solomon of our profession! He was a gentle man, who perceived that our Laws were becoming repressive and extreme, and he set out to soften attitudes a little . . . remind us, if you like, that we are all feeble mortals journeying through life together. His words carried much weight, and throughout my teaching career, I have sought to emulate him. You would call him my role model. Like him I am a great lover of people, and am always keen to understand what makes them tick. I love my pupils, and so they warm to my attitude and are fond of me in return. I am known as Rabban, an affectionate title meaning 'our master' or 'our Great One'.

Now my grandfather believed first and foremost that God was in command of our lives. If we were conscientious in prayer, all our decisions would be his, and we should have nothing to fear. This is the belief on which I too build my life . . .

But why am I explaining all that? What did I start to tell you? Ah yes, the hot-headed young followers of Jesus of Nazareth! Undoubtedly a case for the moderation I was talking about. I have been observing their activities with great interest and – yes, I admit – some alarm. Their influence is now so widespread that it has touched all aspects of city life. What began as a niggling earth tremor rapidly threatens to shake the very foundations of Jerusalem. But where panic sets in – and I think that is the stage my Sadducee colleagues in the Council have reached – where panic sets in, there is particular need for reason and calm. I think there is an element of jealousy creeping in too, which won't do at all.

This crisis is certainly an unusual one and it needs cool handling. Why unusual? Well, do you see these Jesus leaders as dangerous criminals . . . or violent rebels . . . or dagger-waving militants? Of course not! Most are barely educated and would be more at home riding the storms of Lake Galilee than the court of the Sanhedrin. And yet they show gifts of leadership and healing which are rightly appreciated by the people of our city. Some of their cures can only be described as miraculous, and are causing the sick and suffering to be brought from far and wide in the hope of being restored to health.

But the Sanhedrin is not happy . . . Why ever not, you ask, and I have to tell you it is the movement's origin that is in doubt – their power base, if you like. They claim to be led by God's Holy Spirit, and they refuse to budge from their conviction that all their healing is effected through Jesus' name. The boldness of their claims and accusations incenses the Sadducees who believe them to be charlatans, and things reached a climax the other morning. The High Priest – at the end of his tether – had summoned us for a crisis meeting of the full Council. He had arrested the leaders of the Jesus movement the previous day, and locked them in gaol. When they were due to appear before us, lo and behold, it transpired that they had somehow escaped and word came that an angel had led them out. And now – cool as you please – they were preaching in the Temple! When eventually brought before us and challenged as to why they had ignored a ban already imposed on their teaching, they answered with such contemptuous defiance that they would have been condemned to death. But that is when I stepped in. First of all I asked the officers to take the men outside so that we could talk freely – I had no wish to embarrass my colleagues. Then I dared to suggest that, far from punishing them with the ultimate severity, we should let them go free! There was stunned silence! You could have heard a pin drop. But I reasoned that, if God was indeed the inspiration behind this movement, he would win the day anyway, no matter what course we followed. If, however, these 'followers of the Way', as they are called, are pursuing the ramblings of a misguided magician who is no longer with them, his heresies will soon blow away in the wind, and all will return to normal. They listened to me carefully – I was deeply honoured for such respect in what was indeed a desperate moment. And yes, the Jesus followers went free. So that's how it is for the moment.

And now I was pondering the words of a proverb when you first made my acquaintance a few minutes ago. Let me bid you farewell with lines from another of my favourite writings, the Psalms of my ancestor David:

> *He will break the power of the wicked,*
> *but the power of the righteous will be increased.*

BIBLE PASSAGES

Acts 5:33-42

When the members of the Council heard this, they were so furious that they wanted to have the apostles put to death. But one of them, a Pharisee named Gamaliel, who was a teacher of the Law and was highly respected by all the people, stood up in the Council. He ordered the apostles to be taken out for a while, and then he said to the Council, 'Fellow-Israelites, be careful what you do to these men. You remember that Theudas appeared some time ago, claiming to be somebody great, and about four hundred men joined him. But he was killed, all his followers were scattered, and his movement died out.

After that, Judas the Galilean appeared during the time of the census; he drew a crowd after him, but he also was killed, and all his followers were scattered.

And so in this case, I tell you, do not take any action against these men. Leave them alone! If what they have planned and done is of human origin, it will disappear, but if it comes from God, you cannot possibly defeat them. You could find yourselves fighting against God!'

The Council followed Gamaliel's advice. They called the apostles in, had them whipped, and ordered them never again to speak in the name of Jesus; and then they set them free. As the apostles left the Council, they were happy, because God had considered them worthy to suffer disgrace for the sake of Jesus. And every day in the Temple and in people's homes they continued to teach and preach the Good News about Jesus the Messiah.

Proverbs 2:1-15

Learn what I teach you, my son, and never forget what I tell you to do. Listen to what is wise and try to understand it. Yes, beg for knowledge; plead for insight. Look for it as hard as you would for silver or some hidden treasure.

If you do, you will know what it means to fear the Lord and you will succeed in learning about God. It is the Lord who gives wisdom; from him come knowledge and understanding. He provides help and protection for those who are righteous and honest. He protects those who treat others fairly, and guards those who are devoted to him.

If you listen to me, you will know what is right, just, and fair. You will know what you should do. You will become wise, and your knowledge will give you pleasure. Your insight and understanding will protect you and prevent you from doing the wrong thing. They will keep you away from people who stir up trouble by what they say – those who have abandoned a righteous life to live in the darkness of sin, those who find pleasure in doing wrong and who enjoy senseless evil, unreliable people who cannot be trusted.

ADDITIONAL BIBLE REFERENCES FOR PRIVATE STUDY

Acts 5:17-32

Acts 22:2-3

BACKGROUND NOTES

1. Gamaliel's ancestry and authority

Gamaliel – whose name means 'reward of God' – was the son of Simeon . . . possibly the Simeon we read about in Luke's Gospel:

When the parents brought the child Jesus into the Temple to do for him what the Law required, Simeon took the child in his arms and gave thanks to God (Luke 2:27-28).

He was the grandson of the famous Rabbi Hillel, renowned for his wisdom and moderation. Gamaliel continued this tradition, and as the first century AD progressed, his wisdom increased the prestige of the liberal Pharisees and caused them to dominate after the destruction of the Temple in AD70. Two things he achieved personally were the easing of rules governing movement for some groups on the sabbath, and the forbidding of husbands to annul divorce proceedings without their wives' knowledge. He became so highly regarded that the Mishnah (traditional commentary on Hebrew law) drew this conclusion: 'Since Rabban Gamaliel the elder died there has been no more reverence for the law; and purity and abstinence died out at the same time.'

Although he held no particular brief which authorised him to take charge of the Sanhedrin on the occasion of the apostles' arrest, he was clearly able to overturn the Council's thinking by the force of his quiet reasoning and by the respect in which he was held. Three alternatives could have been behind his own attitude on that occasion:

a)   His instinctive desire for tolerance and moderation.

b)   His desire to protect Pharisees from the growing hostility of the Sadducees. Pharisees did have common views with the apostles on such things as resurrection from the dead.

c)   His intuition that he was indeed witnessing the power and Spirit of God at work in this movement. Could he have been a secret believer like – possibly – Nicodemus or Joseph of Arimathea?

2. Pharisees and Sadducees

Rabbi Hillel's descendants represented the realist, liberal and compassionate application of the Jewish Law, as shown by most Pharisees.

The Shammai represented the rigid, harsh, theoretical attitude of the Sadducees, many of whom came from rich and powerful families.

Josephus defines them as follows:

They (Pharisees) ascribe everything to Fate or to God: the decision whether or not to do right rests mainly with men, but in every action Fate takes some part. Every soul is imperishable, but only the souls of good men pass into other bodies, the souls of bad men being subjected to eternal punishment. The Sadducees . . . deny Fate altogether and hold that God is incapable of either committing sin or seeing it; they say that men are free to choose between good and evil, and each individual must decide which he will follow. The permanence of the soul, punishments in Hades, and rewards they deny utterly.

He concludes this definition with this more personal, and quite contemporary-sounding generalisation:

Again, Pharisees are friendly to one another and seek to promote concord with the general public, but Sadducees, even towards each other, show a more disagreeable spirit, and in their relations with men like themselves they are as harsh as they might be to foreigners. This is all I wish to say about the Jewish schools of thought.

In Gamaliel's time the leadership of the Sanhedrin was firmly in the hands of the high priest and the Sadducee party.

3. Theudas and Judas

Gamaliel quotes two historical precedents in the passage from Acts 5 to illustrate the need for circumspect action, and these involve men called Theudas and Judas the Galilean. He tells how both made claims, won supporters, were killed, and faded out. So who were they?

Theudas may have been Theudas the magician who claimed to be a prophet, and persuaded people to follow him to the River Jordan, asserting that he would divide the river by his command. He was caught and beheaded.

Judas may be a Judas who persuaded his compatriots to revolt, saying it would be cowardly to pay taxes to the Romans, submitting to them as lords, when the only lord worthy to receive tributes should be God. This Judas was the forerunner of the zealots.

However there are discrepancies between the various historical records of these two incidents, and scholars are unable to confirm that the timing fits with the characters quoted by Gamaliel.

DISCUSSION TOPICS

1. What characteristics do you see in Gamaliel, and why did the fairly determined Sanhedrin Council pay such attention to him?

2. Do you have any comments to make on his principle that if the matter is not of God it will come to nothing anyway?

3. Are you a better Christian if you are better educated?

4. What advantages/disadvantages do you see in the contribution to church life of
     a) people who have grown up in the faith?
     b) new Christians?

5. Can you suggest ways of interesting and absorbing young people in the life of the church?

6. Is 'communication' an important word in the life of a Christian?

PRAYER
(with words from Ecclesiasticus 2:15-18)

Those who fear the Lord never disobey his words;
And all who love him keep to his ways.

Almighty God, We are sorry for the many times when we have disobeyed you: when we have ignored your teachings, and followed our own desires; when we have neglected or damaged your Creation, in our quest for worldly wealth; when we have disregarded our fellow human beings, and not loved our neighbours as ourselves.

Those who fear the Lord try to do his will;
And all who love him steep themselves in the law.

Almighty God, We pray that you will forgive our mistakes, and show us how to serve you better. Help us to be conscientious in prayer, so that we are open to your guidance; make us eager to learn more about you through the teachings of the Bible and the example of other Christians; may we consider each day wasted if we have not added to our knowledge and understanding of you; give us wisdom to make careful decisions about each step of our lives.

Those who fear the Lord are always prepared;
They humble themselves before him and say:
'We will fall into the hands of the Lord,
Not into the hands of men
For his majesty is equalled by his mercy.'

Almighty God, We want to be your faithful servants. We dedicate our lives to you and ask you to strengthen us for the way ahead. Make us alert to temptation around us and wary of the attractions of an easier life. Reassure us that in your hands we shall be saved through your everlasting mercy and love.

AMEN

PHILIP

I'm in Samaria now, in case you've lost track! All the Jesus followers have had to drop everything, so to speak – and leave Jerusalem. Don't worry, we're in great spirits, but the persecution in the city has reached fever pitch, and we've concluded the Lord is calling us to start his work further afield. As you know, we've had months of niggle and skirmishing with the authorities, but it all came to a head with the horrific murder of our dear friend Stephen. I still can't take it in – stoned to death! I was close to giving up, I'm telling you. But Jesus always made it clear the path would not be easy. I'll tell you what happened in a minute.

But, as I said, here I am in Samaria – not the world's most friendly place and a real challenge if ever there was one! Some of the others are in the countryside around here, the rest are in Judea. Only the apostles stayed behind in the city, God help them. They're constantly in my prayers.

So who am I, you're wondering! My name's Philip. I'd like to be remembered as Philip the Evangelist because I just love preaching and talking to people about Jesus, but I'm new at it so we'll see how I get on! I have a feeling the Holy Spirit has laid a huge opportunity at my door, here in Samaria. Don't confuse me with Philip the apostle from Bethsaida, by the way – I'm not one of the Twelve, never have been. In fact I've only been one of the Jesus leaders for a very short time. It was quite interesting how it happened, and it certainly wasn't the sort of job I was looking for! But any responsibility given to me in the service of God is a bonus as far as I'm concerned.

You've probably heard that the followers were a very happy, caring, loving group of people. They all lived together, sharing everything, looking after each other, and all attending prayers regularly at the Temple. When the Holy Spirit came, the numbers suddenly escalated: one minute we had a hundred and twenty members, and in no time it had grown to about eight thousand! It was thrilling, but, needless to say, that's when the problems started. You see the original group are Jews from the old school, for lack of a better word. They speak Aramaic, and they're very particular about observing all the old traditions in the Temple, and so on. Suddenly we have this influx of Jews who've come from outside the city. Their language is Greek, and they don't have the same strict views about Temple worship. They reckoned they were treated like second-class citizens . . . They probably had a point.

One of the things we've always been good at is providing for the needy – for instance, the widows of our group. To cut a long story short, these newer people felt their widow-women were getting a raw deal. The apostles were ace! They addressed the issue without delay, and set out to appoint seven people to take charge of this poor fund distribution – wise, they must be, and full of the Holy Spirit. Peter and the others could then concentrate on prayer and preaching. As I said, it's a mundane sort of job, but they made it seem important and commissioned us formally with the laying-on of hands. A real perk for me is that I gain access to all sorts of people I wouldn't normally rub shoulders with. It has already taught me a lot. Hopefully I can use the experience now as I try to win the confidence of Samaritan people – they've been our enemies in the past.

But this nightmare of Stephen! I regularly beg the Lord to release me from the horrible visions that torment me. His death was so vile, so barbaric, it's with me every night. Stephen was such a splendid guy. He was one of the seven helpers I've just mentioned . . . young like the rest of us, and yet he had performed amazing miracles and converted crowds of people with his preaching. Sadly his popularity made him enemies, and some despicable characters trumped up stories to get him into trouble. That's not difficult, the way things are, and he ended up in front of the Sanhedrin. He apparently delivered himself of a mammoth speech about our history, to defend himself, but it was punctuated with jibes about the authorities killing Jesus, and it really wound them up. They say he then looked up to heaven and claimed he could see Jesus sitting as the Son of Man at the right hand of God. That finished them off and out he went for stoning.

But you should have seen him! This is what haunts me. As they hurled the stones at him, he was on his knees, and with this wonderful serene expression on his face, he called out to Jesus to forgive them. I can't get it out of my mind. What an example! It has made me determined that whatever lies ahead, it is this sort of courage I must show for the Lord – nothing less is good enough.

That's a grim note to finish on, but don't let it get you down. I'm really raring to go! This is the challenge of my life, friends, and I'm really going for it! I want to meet new people, new races, and transform their lives with the Good News. Watch this space!

BIBLE PASSAGES

Acts 6:1-7

Some time later, as the number of disciples kept growing, there was a quarrel between the Greek-speaking Jews and the native Jews. The Greek-speaking Jews claimed that their widows were being neglected in the daily distribution of funds. So the twelve apostles called the whole group of believers together and said, 'It is not right for us to neglect the preaching of God's word in order to handle finances. So then, brothers and sisters, choose seven men among you who are known to be full of the Holy Spirit and wisdom, and we will put them in charge of this matter. We ourselves, then, will give our full time to prayer and the work of preaching.'

The whole group was pleased with the apostles' proposal, so they chose Stephen, a man full of faith and the Holy Spirit, and Philip, Prochorus, Nicanor, Timon, Parmenas, and Nicolaus, a Gentile from Antioch who had earlier been converted to Judaism. The group presented them to the apostles, who prayed and placed their hands on them.

And so the word of God continued to spread. The number of disciples in Jerusalem grew larger and larger, and a great number of priests accepted the faith.

Acts 7:51-60; Acts 8:1-2

'How stubborn you are!' Stephen went on to say. 'How heathen your hearts, how deaf you are to God's message! You are just like your ancestors: you too have always resisted the Holy Spirit! Was there any prophet that your ancestors did not persecute? They killed God's messengers, who long ago announced the coming of his righteous Servant. And now you have betrayed and murdered him. You are the ones who received God's law, that was handed down by angels – yet you have not obeyed it!'

As the members of the Council listened to Stephen, they became furious and ground their teeth at him in anger. But Stephen, full of the Holy Spirit, looked up to heaven and saw God's glory and Jesus standing at the right-hand side of God. 'Look!' he said. 'I see heaven opened and the Son of Man standing at the right-hand side of God!'

With a loud cry the members of the Council covered their ears with their hands. Then they all rushed at him at once, threw him out of the city, and stoned him. The witnesses left their cloaks in the care of a young man named

Saul. They kept on stoning Stephen as he called out to the Lord, 'Lord Jesus, receive my spirit!' He knelt down and cried out in a loud voice, 'Lord! Do not remember this sin against them!' He said this and died.

And Saul approved of his murder.

That very day the church in Jerusalem began to suffer cruel persecution. All the believers, except the apostles, were scattered throughout the provinces of Judea and Samaria. Some devout men buried Stephen, mourning for him with loud cries.

ADDITIONAL BIBLE REFERENCES FOR PRIVATE STUDY

Acts 6:8-15

Acts 7:1-53

Acts 2:41-47

BACKGROUND NOTES

1. Way of life in the Early Church

The believers in the Early Church were remarkable for their conscientious attention to the teaching of the apostles, their joyful fellowship and sharing together, their corporate worship, and their special meal or Love Feast. It was a meal where everyone brought something according to his or her means, and the food was shared out. Among the early Christians were many freed slaves whose contributions would have been meagre, but this was part of the accepted way of life.

2. Greek-speaking Jews

From the earliest days, evangelism was particularly successful among the Greek-speaking, or Hellenistic Jews, who had probably come to live in Jerusalem from elsewhere. Rigid orthodox Jews tended to look down on them, as their lives had invariably been influenced by different cultures, and they didn't regard the Temple and its practices as their central focus. Many were poor people or former slaves. The Synagogue of Freedmen whose members opposed Stephen's preaching *(Acts 6:9)* consisted of former Jewish slaves who had returned to Palestine from other regions.

Hence as numbers of converts grew, two classes began to emerge among the believers, the Hebrews and the Hellenists. The influx of the latter rapidly put it in the majority, which caused a disproportionate drain on the funds and food supplies, and made this poorer group of newcomers even more unpopular. Their widows may have had fewer family members in the city to support them than the Hebrew widows, which would have increased their need for funds still further.

3. Seven deacons

The twelve apostles acted quickly to resolve the dispute about unfair distribution of the food by asking the group of believers to choose seven representatives to take charge of this. Peter and John saw their own priority as the spreading of the Good News by preaching and teaching, but the duties of these new helpers were practical and administrative. Two of those selected – Philip and Stephen – also had clear preaching gifts, but they were given opportunity to use these in addition to their more mundane tasks. The names of the seven appointed all suggest a Greek background, but most would have been Jewish by birth.

They were officially commissioned with the laying-on of hands and it is interesting to note that, although the apostles had now separated pastoral work from the ministry of the word, yet they considered both required people 'full of the Holy Spirit'. Neither was regarded as inferior. It was not until much later that they were referred to as 'deacons', this title being derived from the Greek word meaning 'to serve' – *diakoneo*.

4. Stephen's speech of defence

Much of Stephen's speech to the Sanhedrin Council consists of a résumé of Israel's history. It was fairly common for Jewish speeches in such circumstances to take this form. Certain aspects of its content, however, were far from the norm, and would have run contrary to the views of traditional Jews. For instance Stephen introduces the idea that much of God's activity has taken place beyond the confines of Palestine, and that wherever God meets his people can be called holy ground. He does not deny God's promise that Abraham's descendants would inherit Palestine, but he preaches against the idea of land being the crucial factor. This opinion would have been like a red rag to the Council bulls. He finally accuses them of failing to recognise any of the leaders God has sent them, and of persecuting them all, the last being Jesus whom they have just killed. That was the last straw for the already-irate Council.

DISCUSSION TOPICS

1. What qualities do you see in Philip and Stephen that would be good for church workers today?

2. Why does a loving God allow someone like Stephen to die at the height of his ministry?

3. The early church loved evangelism; why do we find it so difficult?

4. To what people, and in what areas of society should we target our evangelism?

5. What other ways are there of spreading the Good News?

6. Do big churches have more problems than small churches?

7. When might the art of conciliation be needed in church life?

8. Have you ever accepted a job that was not 'the sort of job I was looking for', as Philip says? Why did you do it and how did it work out?

9. It is not uncommon in our society for people to make up stories which land others in trouble. Where does this happen and what can be done about it?

PRAYER

O God, our heavenly Father, we praise and thank you for all your goodness to us, and particularly for the presence of your Holy Spirit with us on our pilgrimage through life. We want to share this wonderful news with the people around us, but when opportunities occur our tongues so often seem tied. We admire your disciple Philip who, in a hostile world, brought your saving grace to hundreds of people, both Jews and Gentiles. We pray for your strength and guidance to follow his example.

Give us courage to talk about you at times when we might prefer to keep silent, and make us confident that where our faith is strong, words to express it will not be lacking.

Keep us conscientious in prayer and Bible study so that the Gospel we relate is sound and relevant, and give us wisdom to handle the arguments we encounter.

Inspire our witness with infectious enthusiasm so that those who hear our message can't wait to know more.

Above all, teach us how to convey by our actions and attitudes the love which surrounds and uplifts all who turn to you. Through us, may people glimpse the one true Light of the world.

We ask it through Jesus Christ, your Son, our Saviour,

AMEN

SIMON THE SORCERER

Dooby, dooby, doo!
There's magic here for you!
Dooby, dooby, day!
I'll cure you if you pay!
Dooby, dooby, doo!
Just a shekel or two!

Ah, some strangers! The top of the morning to you! Gather round, gather round! Feast your eyes on miracles and marvels, courtesy of Simon, THE GREAT POWER OF GOD! Come closer, good sirs, madam. Have your money ready and witness the power at work!

Don't be shy, give it a try!
Health is here for you to buy!

That's more like it! Bring your suffering ones to the front. Poor dears! Such sad faces everywhere! Cheer up! We'll soon be dancing and singing. But I see new faces, so let me start by showing you my treasures. My old friends know them well – transformed their lives, they did. What would they all do without Simon, their great Power? What, indeed!

Now, over here you see a collection of amulets – all shapes and sizes – everything you could possibly require, to ward off evil spirits and bring you good luck. There are fox teeth and locust eggs to carry when you travel; there are necklaces and statues representing the fertility gods; there are rings and earrings with inscriptions to frighten off evil demons; and the rest are shells and charms with spells written on them. You can look at them more closely later on. Over here in the centre I have the household gods – big ones, small ones; cheap ones, costly ones! Always keep some of those in your homes. Finally, on this side you have Simon's magic clay bowls. For just a small fee, I'll inscribe inside the bowl any saying or incantation you choose, and the luck you need will surely come your way. You can use the bowl for eating if you wish – no problem there.

Hurry now and take your pick!
My power is keen to heal the sick!

Wait a minute! There's something not right here. What have I said? Have I got dirt on my nose? You're just standing there, dumb, like lumps of dead meat! **Come on,** what **is** this? . . . Aha! I know! I know what this is about.

Someone's been telling tales, eh? Someone heard poor Simon getting stick from those bumptious Jews, Peter and his sidekick – is that it? Quite uncalled-for, that. You'd have thought I was competing with his preacher friend, not supporting him! I mean, I even got baptised, didn't I? That showed how impressed I was. No, all I did was ask a harmless question, 'Can I have some of this power you've got so I can give the Holy Spirit to **my** customers too?' Dear me, you'd have thought I'd asked for the clothes off his body! And I'd offered to pay for it too! He just flung at me a whole string of abuse and accusations – the money seemed the thing that maddened him most! Weird!

But I probably need to go back a bit and explain what happened earlier. It started one day when I was quietly setting out my treasures, as I always do. Along comes this chap, Philip, from Jerusalem – didn't look like a Jew and it's not a Jewish name, but that's where he said he was from. Seemed a good, friendly sort of fellow – likeable. He began talking to the people around, and in no time a crowd had gathered. Then all of a sudden he started doing these miraculous healings, and I realised he was some sort of preacher. Would you believe it! On my patch! I was a bit miffed, but I had to hand it to him: he'd really got the Power – the power of God, he called it, and sometimes Jesus Christ. Well, I know all about the Power and I could see he'd got it: evil spirits were roaring out of people, cripples were leaping about, there were things happening everywhere! Now the locals call me the Great Power of God, but I'm telling you – he had it more than me! So I thought I'd get some tips. I did the baptism bit along with all the others, and hung around to observe his technique, and try and copy a few of his spells. Stunning was the only word – I was completely converted!

A bit later on these two characters, Peter and John, turned up from Jerusalem – the heavy brigade, they seemed to be. But give them their due, they were even more impressive. They had this power they called the Holy Spirit which I could sense immediately – made my neck tingle. What they did was to place their hands on the baptised people and wow! You could see the power grip them! Well, I figured I could make good use of that Holy Spirit power. I could have added it to my treasures and done great work for the people here – long after those characters have gone on their way. So that's when I asked if I could buy it. Believe it or not, this Peter fellow told me to go to hell, if you please! Fat cheek – and them foreigners too! But it was an opportunity not to be missed, so I ignored the rudeness, and with my natural charm I asked them to pray for me. Unfortunately they disappeared back to Jerusalem a few days later so I never got any further. And now I seem to have lost half my customers as well!

Roll up, roll up!

Dooby, dooby, dower!
I'm the greatest Power!
Dooby, dooby, double moon!
Holy Spirit coming soon!

BIBLE PASSAGE

Acts 8:5-25

Philip went to the principal city in Samaria and preached the Messiah to the people there. The crowds paid close attention to what Philip said, as they listened to him and saw the miracles that he performed. Evil spirits came out from many people with a loud cry, and many paralysed and lame people were healed. So there was great joy in that city.

A man named Simon lived there, who for some time had astounded the Samaritans with his magic. He claimed that he was someone great, and everyone in the city, from all classes of society, paid close attention to him. 'He is that power of God known as "The Great Power",' they said. They paid this attention to him because for such a long time he had astonished them with his magic. But when they believed Philip's message about the Good News of the Kingdom of God and about Jesus Christ, they were baptised, both men and women. Simon himself also believed; and after being baptised, he stayed close to Philip and was astounded when he saw the great wonders and miracles that were being performed.

The apostles in Jerusalem heard that the people of Samaria had received the word of God, so they sent Peter and John to them. When they arrived, they prayed for the believers that they might receive the Holy Spirit. For the Holy Spirit had not yet come down on any of them; they had only been baptised in the name of the Lord Jesus. Then Peter and John placed their hands on them, and they received the Holy Spirit.

Simon saw that the Spirit had been given to the believers when the apostles placed their hands on them. So he offered money to Peter and John, and said, 'Give this power to me too, so that anyone I place my hands on will receive the Holy Spirit.'

But Peter answered him, 'May you and your money go to hell, for thinking that you can buy God's gift with money! You have no part or share in our work, because your heart is not right in God's sight. Repent, then, of this evil plan of yours, and pray to the Lord that he will forgive you for thinking such a thing as this. For I see that you are full of bitter envy and are a prisoner of sin.'

Simon said to Peter and John, 'Please pray to the Lord for me, so that none of these things you spoke of will happen to me.'

After they had given their testimony and proclaimed the Lord's message, Peter and John went back to Jerusalem.

ADDITIONAL BIBLE REFERENCES FOR PRIVATE STUDY

Acts 16:16-23

John 2:23-25

BACKGROUND NOTES

1. Magicians etc

Magicians, astrologers and soothsayers were a common phenomenon in the ancient world. Throughout history people have recognised that there are forces at work which cannot be seen or touched. Failing any religious belief to account for them, people ignorant of science and the natural world turn easily to superstition and magic. Even those of us with a firm faith in God have been known to avoid Friday 13th or throw salt over our shoulders!

Magicians in New Testament times were quite influential, respected members of the community, who earned a comfortable living through their services.

So what did they offer? They would certainly have sold amulets, charms, magic bowls and the other items mentioned in Simon's script, all of which would promise cures or protection against the powers of evil. In addition there was widespread use of spells and incantations, which Josephus tells us were even used by the great Solomon himself. Moreover there were various practices for predicting the future, such as reading an animal's liver, or mixing liquids and interpreting the shapes created. A Babylonian favourite was to shake arrows, throw them down and then interpret the pattern on the ground. Finally, astrology was popular, despite its condemnation by Old Testament writers:

Do not follow the ways of other nations;
do not be disturbed by unusual sights in the sky,
even though other nations are terrified.
The religion of these people is worthless (Jeremiah 10:2).

It would be harsh to judge these magicians as conscious frauds or villains. Most would genuinely believe in the powers they claimed to exercise. 'Deluded' is the word we might use to describe them.

1. Simon the Sorceror's legacies

The dictionary defines *simony* as the buying or selling of ecclesiastical privileges or preferment.   In more general terms the word can refer to unworthily turning things spiritual into things commercial, or as John Stott puts it, *'to traffic in the things of God'*. It was vigorously denounced by the Church, but was particularly widespread in the Middle Ages. Legal measures were taken against it as late as 1898. Its origin is this action by Simon – described as sinful – in Acts 8.

But just how great a sinner was Simon? When he heard Philip's message, he declared, along with the others, that he was a believer and wished to be baptised. His motives at that stage appeared dubious on account of the money interest, but he then went on to observe Peter and John laying hands on the believers and imparting the Holy Spirit. He clearly recognised the power of the Holy Spirit, and acknowledged it to be something greater than his own powers – quite an admission for a famous local magician. Peter still saw him as motivated by greed *('You have no part or share in our work, because your heart is not right in God's sight', Acts 8:21)*, but a few minutes later his request for prayer could suggest genuine repentance. Since no-one who seeks to follow Christ is perfect, are we to assume he was more *'a prisoner of sin'* than the rest of us?

Needless to say, much has been written about this intriguing character over the centuries – almost all of it legend or supposition. One of the most influential early writers was the second-century Christian, Justin Martyr, who was himself a Samaritan, converted from paganism. He identifies our Simon as Simon Magus, a famous magician from the Samarian town of Gitta, who founded a school of magic at Alexandria, and made people believe he could fly! Justin Martyr appears to accept that Simon and his followers were basically Christian, but were the originators of various misguided and heretical beliefs. After his death Simon was credited with being the founder of the heresy Gnosticism, which claims that only a chosen few are singled out for enlightenment. Simon is said to have been worshipped, himself, as the highest

God, by his countrymen – a situation which would bear out the apostle Peter's misgivings about his intentions. Another second-century piece of writing, the apocryphal book *Acts of St Peter* has lengthy tales of Simon Magus corrupting Roman Christians with his heresies, and being put in his place by Peter who on every occasion exceeded his prowess with superior deeds of magic!

The most likely conclusion, therefore, is that Simon was genuinely impressed by the signs and wonders of the Holy Spirit, but failed to take the next step of personal commitment to Jesus the Saviour.

2. Jews and Samaritans

Well-known Bible stories like the Good Samaritan leave us in no doubt as to the animosity that existed between the Jews and Samaritans, but where did it come from? And how was it possible for Philip to preach in Samaria if there were no dealings between the two? *cf. The woman answered, 'You are a Jew, and I am a Samaritan – so how can you ask me for a drink?' (Jews will not use the same cups and bowls that Samaritans use.) John 4:9.*

The quarrel between them was an ancient one, dating from the break-up of the monarchy after Solomon's death in the tenth century BC, when ten tribes defected and only two remained loyal to Jerusalem. It became entrenched in the eighth century BC when the Assyrians conquered the northern region of Samaria, deported twenty-seven thousand Israelites, and populated the area with foreigners. The remaining Israelites intermarried with the newcomers. Two centuries later the Babylonians behaved in the same way, but with the southern region of Jerusalem – but this time the displaced Jews stubbornly maintained their identity. When they finally returned to their homeland, these Jews were contemptuous of the northerners who, having intermarried and become mixed race, appeared to them no better than heathens. Things went from bad to worse when in the fourth century BC the Samaritans built a rival temple. And so it continued.

To preach in the face of a thousand years of dispute was a momentous step for Philip, and the real start of the Early Church's mission to the 'outside world'. Philip was clearly a splendid evangelist, but the Samaritans had already been looking for a messiah so this may explain why they were so responsive to his message. Moreover the power of his preaching about the Kingdom of God and its realisation through the name of Jesus the Messiah were amply borne out by the efficacy of Philip's miraculous deeds.

DISCUSSION TOPICS

1. What do you think of Simon and his conversion?

2. If you had met him, do you think you would have liked him?

3. What place do astrology and superstition play in our lives?

4. Are they wicked?

5. The National Lottery has provided funding for many worthy projects. Do you consider this a benefit for society or are you unhappy about the source of the money?

6. Do 'signs and wonders' still happen today?

7. Do we have any right to decide whether a person's commitment to Christ is genuine or not?

PRAYER

Teach us, good Lord, to serve thee as thou deservest;
To give and not to count the cost;
To fight and not to heed the wounds;
To toil and not to seek for rest;
To labour and not to ask for any reward
Save that of knowing that we do thy will.

Ignatius Loyola (1491-1556)

THE ETHIOPIAN EUNUCH

Welcome, good people, to the kingdom of Meroe and palace of our honoured Candace! Please be seated, and I'll try to give you a résumé of the momentous events of my recent trip. I would spend all day with you, but her majesty the Queen-mother has been without her Chancellor for several weeks due to my holiday, and affairs of state are pressing. So here – as briefly as I can manage – is my life-changing experience, for that is certainly what it was. As Isaiah said, *'Who would have believed what we now report? Who could have seen the Lord's hand in this?'*

First, a personal word about myself. I would not embarrass you with personal trivia, but this detail is relevant to my tale. It is customary for male officials at the Queen's court to be castrated, so that is my situation. It follows that I am precluded by Jewish Law from being part of the Jewish congregation. Nevertheless I have for some time been an interested adherent. There have been Jews here in Meroe for centuries, and I've enjoyed many a stimulating discussion on matters of their faith. With its good moral standards Judaism has much to commend it in an era where gods are two a penny and society reaps no benefit from any of them. I'm sorry if such detail offends you, but you need to understand my state of mind as I embarked on this adventure. I attended the local synagogue regularly and spent much time poring over the scriptures, but I was still searching for I know not what. I prayed for something to satisfy this yearning.

What better than to make a pilgrimage to Jerusalem, the great heart of it all? Long-distance routes cross at Meroe, and it always abounds with caravans and travellers. There is no shortage of chat about exciting experiences, and the atmosphere is infectious. Once the thought had entered my head, I couldn't wait to be on my way. What did I expect? I cannot say – perhaps it was a hope that this God I so much wanted to worship might reveal himself to me if I went in search of him. And, of course, he did . . . but later on.

Jerusalem was greatly to my liking – a bustling, vibrant city, breath-taking in the beauty of its buildings. The picturesque steep hilly streets thronged with people and animals of every description. There were fair-skinned infants with gleaming eyes, and wizened crones bent double with suffering; there were sumptuous robes and filthy rags; there were noisy traders with carpets of colourful wares, and quiet scholars with eager pupils in a huddle – a rich mosaic of human life. As I was borne along by the crowds, I was witness to numerous little incidents: thieving children being chased and screamed at, stray dogs knocking over bursting pomegranates, doves soaring in a flutter, a Pharisee and his students reciting from David's Psalm:

When I look at the sky, which you have made,
At the moon and the stars, which you set in their places –
What are human beings, that you think of them; mere mortals that you care for them?

Last, but by no means least, I vividly remember a handful of rough-looking young men with fiery eyes, addressing onlookers about a hero they claimed was the Messiah – a man called Jesus of Nazareth, apparently put to death by the authorities. Even as I watched, some Sanhedrin officials approached and the people scattered like lightning into the maze of tiny streets.

A rich mosaic indeed, and yet, friends, there seemed no tile in it for me. As I left Jerusalem my heart was empty. I had prayed to the Jewish God, I had offered worship in his holy city. The psalmist says, '*At sunrise I offer my prayer and wait for your answer*', but for me no answer came.

I had managed to obtain a scroll of the writings of the prophet Isaiah – an excellent companion for the long journey home. I opened it and was immediately engrossed. As we clattered along the desert road to Gaza, I was reading aloud, already oblivious to my surroundings. My mind harked back to that group of ardent Jesus-followers, and so I picked some lines which seemed appropriate, about the Lord's servant. I paused at a curious paragraph: the Lord apparently said his servant would succeed in his task and would be highly honoured, but Isaiah continues that he was punished and ill-treated and had nothing to say for himself. Would nations marvel and kings be speechless with amazement at such a pathetic figure? I read it out again: '*He never said a word . . .*' Suddenly I heard a noise above the rattle of my carriage wheels – the sound of pounding footsteps and harsh breathing. I started up quickly, expecting trouble. Imagine my astonishment at seeing a pleasant-faced young man jogging along beside me. 'Can you understand that?' he asked in Greek. Was he impertinent? Instinctively I knew he was not. I invited him to jump up and join me in the carriage. He said his name was Philip. Then followed the most illuminating conversation of my life.

He answered my queries, explaining that Isaiah had the suffering Jewish Remnant in mind, but that Jesus of Nazareth himself quoted these words. Jesus said the servant's suffering foretold the humiliation and death **he** would have to endure for God's plan to be fulfilled. Philip explained all about God's Kingdom and this Messiah Jesus. I was enthralled. Of course **this** was the exciting news being imparted to those crowds in the alleys of Jerusalem.

Philip told me that God's Holy Spirit had instructed him to chase after me, but somehow I already knew! God was answering my prayer, not in Jerusalem, but here, through this stranger, on the bleak Gaza road. My heart leapt with happiness! This was my new life, and I wanted it to begin at once. We drove past some water, and on my request, we stopped for Philip to baptise me.

So here I am, friends, a new man! I am delighted to be home in our glorious kingdom – I hope you will take time to visit it. Being at the confluence of rivers means we have golden cornfields and lush date palms; moreover our coffers are brimming with the gold, ivory and precious stones that abound here – my work as state treasurer presents no problems! But all this pales before the immeasurable blessing of my experience with God. I want all my countrymen to share it!

BIBLE PASSAGES

Acts 8:26-39

An angel of the Lord said to Philip, 'Get ready and go south to the road that goes from Jerusalem to Gaza.' (This road is not used nowadays.) So Philip got ready and went. Now an Ethiopian eunuch, who was an important official in charge of the treasury of the queen of Ethiopia, was on his way home. He had been to Jerusalem to worship God and was going back home in his carriage. As he rode along, he was reading from the book of the prophet Isaiah. The Holy Spirit said to Philip, 'Go over to that carriage and stay close to it.' Philip ran over and heard him reading from the book of the prophet Isaiah. He asked him, 'Do you understand what you are reading?'

The official replied, 'How can I understand unless someone explains it to me?' And he invited Philip to climb up and sit in the carriage with him. The passage of scripture which he was reading was this:

'Like a sheep that is taken to be slaughtered,
like a lamb that makes no sound when its wool is cut off,
he did not say a word.
He was humiliated, and justice was denied him.
No one will be able to tell about his descendants,
Because his life on earth has come to an end.'

The official asked Philip, 'Tell me, of whom is the prophet saying this? Of himself or of someone else?' Then Philip began to speak; starting from this passage of scripture, he told him the Good News about Jesus. As they travelled down the road, they came to a place where there was some water, and the official said, 'Here is some water. What is to keep me from being baptised?'

The official ordered the carriage to stop, and both Philip and the official went down into the water, and Philip baptised him. When they came up out of the water, the Spirit of the Lord took Philip away. The official did not see him again, but continued on his way, full of joy.

Isaiah 53:1-10

The people reply,
'Who would have believed what we now report?
Who could have seen the Lord's hand in this?
It was the will of the Lord that his servant
should grow like a plant taking root in dry ground.
He had no dignity or beauty to make us take notice of him.
There was nothing attractive about him, nothing that would draw us to him.
We despised him and rejected him; he endured suffering and pain.
No one would even look at him – we ignored him as if he were nothing.

But he endured the suffering that should have been ours, the pain that we should have borne.
All the while we thought that his suffering was punishment sent by God.
But because of our sins he was wounded, beaten because of the evil we did.
We are healed by the punishment he suffered, made whole by the blows he received.
All of us were like sheep that were lost, each of us going his own way.
But the Lord made the punishment fall on him, the punishment all of us deserved.

He was treated harshly, but endured it humbly;
he never said a word.
Like a lamb about to be slaughtered, like a sheep about to be sheared,
he never said a word.
He was arrested and sentenced and led off to die, and no one cared about his fate.
He was put to death for the sins of our people.
He was placed in a grave with the wicked, he was buried with the rich,
Even though he had never committed a crime or ever told a lie.'

The Lord says,
'It was my will that he should suffer;
his death was a sacrifice to bring forgiveness.
And so he will see his descendants;
he will live a long life, and through him my purpose will succeed.'

ADDITIONAL BIBLE REFERENCES FOR PRIVATE STUDY

Psalm 68:28-33

Isaiah 11:10-12

BACKGROUND NOTES

1. Ethiopia

Ethiopia has had a variety of meanings over the centuries, having been used to denote Africa south of Egypt, Arabia and even India. Sometimes it has had a vague meaning suggesting peoples from a long way off. The Greek poet Homer thought of Ethiopians as the most distant tribes on earth who lived where the sun set.

At the time Luke was writing, however, Ethiopia was clearly limited to land south of Egypt, between Aswan and Khartoum, and in particular the kingdom of Meroe at the confluence of the Rivers Nile and Tacassi. Ancient geographers sometimes described this area as an island. Now it would be part of Sudan, not Ethiopia.

Meroe was a wealthy kingdom, and its capital was a flourishing caravan centre and hub of cultural, economic and political activity. Numerous languages including Greek would have been spoken.

2. Candace

This was not a personal name. Like 'Pharaoh' or 'Caesar' it was a generic title, and refers to a queen-mother ruling the country on behalf of her son. The king himself was revered more as a god, and was considered too holy to perform affairs of state!

3. Acts 8:33

For observant readers who wonder why this verse does not tally with Isaiah 53:8, the answer is that the Acts quotation comes from the Greek (Septuagint) Text, whereas our Old Testament comes from the slightly different Hebrew (Massoretic) Text.

4. Baptism

The eunuch was keen to be baptised because it was by baptism and circumcision that a Gentile entered the Jewish faith. He would view baptism by immersion as the appropriate way of demonstrating commitment to Jesus whom he had come to realise was the promised Messiah.

Baptism symbolised three things for the early Christians:

a) It washed the person clean in preparation for receiving God's grace.

b) It marked a complete break from the former life.

c) It showed union with Christ for as the candidate went under the water he died with Christ, and as he came up again he rose with Christ. (*'By our baptism, then, we were buried with him and shared his death, in order that, just as Christ was raised from death by the glorious power of the Father, so also we might live a new life'*, Romans 6:4.)

5. Luke's interest in the story

Luke would have thought this story significant for several reasons:

a) It represented another leap forward in the development of Christian mission from the strict confines of Judaism to the Gentile world – the door to Africa was now open. Although no facts are known about the eunuch's subsequent Christian activity, we can assume an influential, scholarly man with such enthusiasm would hardly keep his experiences to himself.

b) This account shows God taking active control of Philip's ministry to the Gentiles, even arranging the details of how it should occur.

c) It shows another of Philip's many gifts as a disciple and evangelist. He has already been a tactful administrator and a charismatic crowd-puller. Here his gift is that of personal empathy with a single individual . . . and one who is high-ranking and from a foreign country – quite a challenge!

d) Through the reference to Isaiah 53 Luke could highlight Jesus' comment that he would have to suffer for God's purpose to be fulfilled according to the prophets. Luke clearly regarded this fulfilment of prophecy as important, and referred to it at other times.

DISCUSSION TOPICS

1. Have you had experience of God
   a) answering your prayers?
   b) having plans for your life?

2. What sort of things can act as stumbling blocks for people considering the Christian way of life?

3. Why do we choose to be baptised?

4. The eunuch's meeting with Philip suddenly made him eager to share the Good News. What sort of things might he have wanted to tell his people?

5. Is it easy for the leading politicians of our country to be practising Christians?

6. Would strangers or people in less conventional circumstances feel at home in your church?

7. If Christians feel the Lord calling them to preach, how necessary is it for them to complete a course of study and examination?

8 Can anything be done to bridge the gap between rich and poor countries?

9 Could you, like the eunuch, describe your community as one where 'gods are two a penny and society reaps no benefit from any of them'?

10 Does our society have 'good moral standards'?

PRAYER

Dear God, We have been inspired and spurred to action by the activities of the Jerusalem believers who, two thousand years ago, brought your Church into being.

We thank you for Philip, who converted an Ethiopian chancellor with the good news that Jesus had died to bring forgiveness for his sins – news he had been searching for, and news which transformed his life.

We ask you to bless and equip us, who are your Church of today. Make us effective disciples and prosper our mission to spread your Gospel throughout the world.

May our message be faithful to your teaching, but relevant to the needs of our world;

May we be forward-looking, embracing the new trends of the twenty-first century whilst holding fast to the essentials of the past; give us the wisdom to make these choices.

Make us courageous in the face of opposition or ridicule, and persuasive in our witnessing to your eternal presence and power; may the voice of the Church be influential in the affairs of government;

Above all, make us your worthy ambassadors:
Offering peace in place of discord;
welcoming all who approach the threshold;
leading those who seek towards your Kingdom;
proclaiming your promise of love and salvation to all people and races.

We ask this through Jesus Christ our Lord,

AMEN

DORCAS

'You silly child! You're lucky to be alive!'
If mama said this once, she said it a thousand times! . . . not so much to me, it was usually my cousins. You see, we lived here in Joppa, near the sea, and the boys were always getting into scrapes – accidents on the boats, falling in the water, anything you can think of! Or sometimes they'd hurt themselves with their slings or spears when they went off to chase wild animals. We were for ever washing their wounds and patching them up. Then off they would go again! 'You're lucky to be alive!' was what mama always said. I never gave it a thought at the time – it was just one of those things mothers say. But I've suddenly had to rethink, my dears! I'll never take those words lightly again. You see, it happened to **me**! – last week – but not just a silly bang on the head or cut knee . . . I actually died! Really and truly! I was lying there dead, and Peter – you know, the wonderful leader of the followers of the Way, from Jerusalem – well, that Peter brought me back to life again. Of course, mama was misguided when she called it 'lucky'; there was no luck about me being alive – it was the hand of God; Peter prayed to him and the prayer was answered. But we often talk about the good Lord like that, don't we?

I'm still very hazy about what happened. I'd been rushing around rather stupidly – you know how it is! As you get older there seems to be more to do, not less! Several families in the street have had a really **awful** time with sickness – I give them a hand where I can – and two or three of my old people can't get out and about at all now. If I'm not around there with my baskets of bread or clean washing, they're in a real fix. I hope you won't think I'm complaining, my dears. It's what I love doing – it's my life. But I will admit I've not been feeling so great these last few months – nothing you could put your finger on but – you know – tired when I shouldn't be, bit dizzy, not hungry for my meals, windy pains afterwards – oh how embarrassing! You've all been the same, I'm quite sure.

Then on this particular day I should have been at dear Deborah's to help bath the new baby – she only has one arm, poor Deborah – but I just couldn't manage it! It was awful of me but I could not get myself up. And that was it – my number was up! I shut my eyes and there were all these flashing lights . . . and that was it! The next thing I knew was this man's voice saying, 'Tabitha, get up!' (That's my name in Hebrew, Tabitha). I opened my eyes and there was this huge gentleman, Peter, kneeling beside me, staring hard at me. He took my hands and helped me up into my chair, then he went off downstairs to tell everyone I was better.

As I sat there on my own, I had this simply **heavenly** feeling of being held in a really warm embrace – just like it was with dear mama when we were children. Does that sound silly? I'm not very good with words – they're not my forte. But there is no doubt at all in my mind – that presence was Almighty God, right here in the room with me. What a privilege to experience such a thing! I shall always be grateful for such blessings.

To go back to the story, Peter went to tell everyone, as I said, and my goodness gracious! There were kind friends from all over the town! Of course, they had really come to pay their respects at my burial – what a shock they must have had! Even in that incredible moment of seeing them pour into the room, I had a little weep because the widows were all dressed in the clothes I made them! I couldn't help but notice because the fabrics are all so special. I have a little money, d'you see, and I specially like to make little luxuries for these poor people who have suffered so much.

In case you wonder how I come to make so many clothes, that's something else I owe to mama. We were a devout Jewish family and she brought us up very strictly – we were all made to be hard-working and helpful. The boys worked in the fields or went out fishing and hunting, and I learnt to weave and sew. There were many people in Joppa who were handy with the loom and the needle – the town was quite known for it – so it was natural for me to practise these skills. Mama took it a step further. 'Now you have reached a good standard,' she would say, pointing her finger at me, 'You must make yourself useful! Use your gifts to help people. That's what the good book says!' So she would instruct me to take a pretty shawl along to the poor old lady at the harbour, and I was told to make her a nice drink at the same time. That's how I developed my liking for making clothes for everyone.

There's another little thing that might be of interest. My parents gave me the name Dorcas which means 'gazelle', an animal known for its grace and beauty. Mama's friends would come up to me and say 'Here's our little beauty!' or 'You'll have to stay slim and pretty with a name like that!' You know the absurd things people say to children. Well, as I got older it worried me because I knew for certain that I'd never be particularly nice-looking. So I resolved to create beauty in my daily life, so that the Lord would be pleased with me and I'd not let him down – silly, wasn't it? But the last few days I've been listening to Peter's wonderful news about Jesus of Nazareth and what he did, and I realise I wasn't silly at all. He was the Messiah, and yet all his life was spent loving and serving people. He will be my model from now on, and I mean to work even harder for his sake . . . I'd better be careful not to overdo it and die again too quickly, though!

BIBLE PASSAGES

Acts 9:36-42

In Joppa there was a woman named Tabitha, who was a believer. (Her name in Greek is Dorcas, meaning 'a deer'.) She spent all her time doing good and helping the poor. At that time she became ill and died. Her body was washed and laid in a room upstairs. Joppa was not very far from Lydda, and when the believers in Joppa heard that Peter was in Lydda, they sent two men to him with the message, 'Please hurry and come to us.' So Peter got ready and went with them. When he arrived, he was taken to the room upstairs, where all the widows crowded round him, crying and showing him all the shirts and coats that Dorcas had made while she was alive. Peter put them all out of the room, and knelt down and prayed; then he turned to the body and said, 'Tabitha, get up!' She opened her eyes, and when she saw Peter, she sat up. Peter reached over and helped her get up. Then he called all the believers, including the widows, and presented her alive to them. The news about this spread all over Joppa, and many people believed in the Lord.

Luke 8:49-56

While Jesus was saying this, a messenger came from the official's house. 'Your daughter has died,' he told Jairus; 'don't bother the Teacher any longer.' But Jesus heard it and said to Jairus, 'Don't be afraid; only believe, and she will be well.'
When he arrived at the house, he would not let anyone go in with him except Peter, John, and James, and the child's father and mother. Everyone there was crying and mourning for the child. Jesus said, 'Don't cry; the child is not dead – she is only sleeping!'
They all laughed at him, because they knew that she was dead. But Jesus took her by the hand and called out, 'Get up, my child!' Her life returned, and she got up at once, and Jesus ordered them to give her something to eat. Her parents were astounded, but Jesus commanded them not to tell anyone what had happened.

Deuteronomy 10:17-19

The Lord your God is supreme over all gods and over all powers. He is great and mighty, and he is to be feared. He does not show partiality, and he does not accept bribes. He makes sure that orphans and widows are treated fairly; he loves the foreigners who live with our people, and gives them food and clothes. So then, show love for those foreigners, because you were once foreigners in Egypt.

ADDITIONAL BIBLE REFERENCES FOR PRIVATE STUDY

Matthew 20:26-28

Matthew 25:31-40

Proverbs 31:10-30

BACKGROUND NOTES

1. Lydda and Joppa

Lydda (or Lod) is an outer suburb of Tel Aviv – now the location of Tel Aviv international airport – and Joppa (Jaffa) is a coastal district of the same city. These would have been separate towns ten miles apart in Dorcas' day. Joppa, which possessed the only natural harbour on the Mediterranean for many miles, had been the seaport for Jerusalem until Herod the Great built the magnificent new port of Caesarea. Joppa is perched high on a rock which juts out into the sea.

Right from earliest times the town had a reputation for skill in leather, wood and metal crafts.

Peter's mission was successful in Lydda and Joppa and a thriving Christian community developed in this area.

2. A girl's upbringing

At the time of the Early Church, Jewish men were still considered in most respects superior to women. Boys of the family would attend the synagogue school, and be instructed by their father in a trade. Girls were largely the mother's responsibility, and were trained by her in all the skills of keeping a home and family. They certainly did not aspire to a career outside the home. Baking, spinning and weaving were the order of the day, but girls were also taught to be unselfish, helpful and supportive to their elders and to the needy. Both sexes learned to be hard-working and disciplined, and to have a deep reverence for God. The bonds of family life were very strong, as they still are today in Jewish families.

Beauty was important to women, and jewellery, make-up, perfume and hairstyling all played a part in their daily lives. The scriptures warned, however, that there were two types of beauty: outer beauty and inner beauty of personality (*'Beauty in a woman without good judgement is like a gold ring in a pig's snout', Proverbs 11:22*).

We have no description of Dorcas' appearance and nothing further is known about her except the few verses from Acts 9, but the word 'believer' in verse 36 is interesting: the Greek word used here was the word for 'disciple', and this is the only time the feminine form of the word is used in the New Testament. Dorcas must have been known as an active worker for the Jesus cause.

3. Clothing

Most Jewish men of this period wore a close-fitting inner garment or shirt, an outer cloak or coat, and sandals. The shirt was made of wool, linen or cotton, and the outer garment was usually wool to wrap round the body for warmth. It could be used as a bed cover at night. Rich men might have expensive silk or linen coats with wide sleeves and fringes.

Women's clothes were similar to men's, but longer – being worn right down to the ankles. The shirt would probably have a V-neck and be embroidered along the edges. No doubt the talents of Dorcas would be in evidence here. Women also wore squares of material, fastened with cord, on their heads.

In order to make these clothes, the women had first to prepare the fabric. The preparation of woollen material involved first washing the wool, then combing it. After that it was spun into lengths on a special wooden stick. Next – after further washing – came the dyeing process. Dyes were made from crushed shells, fruit or lice eggs – these being mixed with water. Finally it was woven on a simple wooden loom, often used outdoors.

4. Luke the doctor

Throughout his writing Luke showed the doctor's interest in medical matters, and healing in particular. Considering the raising of Dorcas is narrated in only seven verses of Acts, we learn a surprising amount of detail. Firstly we are shown how Peter models his action on Jesus' healing of Jairus' daughter: as on that occasion, the room is cleared of mourners and spectators, and Peter prepares himself alone. When he addresses the body, he uses almost identical words to Jesus; in fact, it has been pointed out that, if Peter was speaking Aramaic on this occasion as he did once or twice, only one letter would have been different: Jesus said, *'Talitha koum!'*; Peter would have said, *'Tabitha koum!'*

Peter also used the same word of command, 'Get up!' It is interesting that the verb used here – *anistemi* – is also the verb used of God raising Jesus from death, which calls to mind the new life which we can all enjoy through the power of the resurrection.

Finally Luke is careful to mention Peter's time of prayer before the healing, thus reminding the reader that the miracle was achieved not through Peter's power, but God's. No doubt the people of Joppa had sent for Peter with the express intention of having Dorcas restored to life, but as far as we know, this was a 'first' for Peter. He would have felt an even greater need than usual of reassurance and guidance from his Lord.

DISCUSSION TOPICS

1. What difference do you think the news of Jesus made to the life of Dorcas?

2. How do we answer people who say they lead good lives and have no need of religion?

3. Are we better or worse at instilling good values in our children nowadays?

4. How is the teaching of Jesus evident in
   a) the life of your church?
   b) your own daily life?

5. Would you always take the view that people are lucky to be alive?

6. Can you describe any experience of the presence of God in your life?

7. Are there any ways in which you try to create beauty in your life?

8. Many churches have a small proportion of members who rush around doing most of the work and a larger proportion who play a less active role. Are there any answers to this problem?

PRAYER

Dear Father God, we learn about Dorcas as the lady in the Bible who was 'full of good works', spending her time caring for the sick and needy, and making clothes for the poor. We thank you for Dorcas, and for all those in the world today who devote their lives to serving and helping others:

We thank you for families where, from the earliest, we are loved despite our faults, and cared for despite our inability to pay.
May we never take our homes for granted, but learn eagerly how to be the home-makers of the future.

We thank you for those responsible for education, health and welfare.
Give them knowledge, strength and patience for their work, and the reward of knowing they are walking in the shoes of Jesus Christ, the greatest teacher and healer.

We thank you for all who work to make our communities safe, comfortable and orderly: for police and emergency services, local government and council workers and those in public transport.
Help us to recognise and value their contribution, and show concern for countries who do not know such benefits.

We thank you for those who govern and hold positions of responsibility in our land.
Give them wisdom and inspired leadership, and make their decisions just, compassionate and relevant.

Lord, you have instructed us to love our neighbours. As we remember all these people who serve, we pray that you will equip us for our own contribution. By the power of your Holy Spirit, may we lead those around us to a greater understanding of you and of your Kingdom.

AMEN

CAPTAIN CORNELIUS

Good afternoon, ladies and gentlemen! Welcome to Caesarea! I don't suppose you often visit a Roman garrison, but you couldn't find a better one – King Herod saw to that! And our crack Italian regiment is the real *crème de la crème*! It's super-efficient, with equipment second to none – but you could say that of most Roman divisions. I'm just a centurion here – that means I'm responsible for a hundred men – quite a handful sometimes, but it's a great life. I wouldn't change it!

But you haven't come here to listen to eulogies about the regiment! As you've obviously heard, this has been a week of drama – and I don't mean fighting and campaigning. As far in the opposite direction as you could go, in fact! Yet it's fair to say the events have taken Caesarea by storm. Crowds have joined the followers of Jesus. Never known a recruiting campaign like it!

I still can't believe it all centred on me! Spent hours mulling it over on night duty, and I figure it must be because I'm a God-fearing man – I've been that ever since I came to Caesarea; I'm telling you I was sick to death of the profusion of silly gods we had. Nobody took them seriously and the state of our society proved it – corrupt as anything, it was. When I came here and saw how the Jews lived: worshipping their one true God, praying to him daily, living good lives according to his laws – I reckoned they'd got it right. All my family felt the same – not just me. Couldn't become Jews, of course, but we've done the next best thing and followed their way of life. We've been enriched; I know it was the right decision.

What I've come round to thinking, though, is that God must have chosen me because of this; perhaps he wanted to show Peter and the others that Gentiles like us have something to offer. But was it odd the way it started!

It was a week ago. Had the fright of my life! This angel suddenly appeared in front of me! It wasn't night-time, like a dream or something. It was three o'clock in the afternoon; I was having my usual prayer time. Then this dazzling figure appeared – couldn't mistake it was an angel. Fair knocked me back, it did. I mean, I don't have a problem with angels – we know God acts in all sorts of strange ways. But to have it happen to you – right there in your room in broad daylight! . . . well, unnerving, to put it mildly!

He was very pleasant; didn't waste any time about his business. Told me quickly that God was pleased with what I was doing – I was encouraged by that when it sank in afterwards – would I send my men to Joppa to find this chap called Simon Peter! Said where to find him and that was it! So I didn't waste any time either. By lunch-time next day one of my men and two servants were thirty miles down the coast. Had a spot of trouble finding the place . . . a tanner's house – bit unusual place for a Jew to stay, with their rules about unclean and so on – but in the event, that was the whole point of the exercise. I'll explain in a minute. So they found the place, but Peter didn't ask them in – seemed preoccupied, 'a bit spaced', my man said! But when they gave my message he got his act together, invited them for the night, and made plans for an early start the next day. Got six of his mates to come along as well – maybe in case it was a trap, I don't know.

So I invited my family and friends round – to hear God's message. It was strange as we waited – everyone was excited, some were scared, was it something good or was it bad? I was sure it must be good from what the angel said about God being pleased with me. But you never know! Only four days in all before they got here, but it seemed longer; I was nervous by the time I welcomed them in – fell down on my knees, I did, as though it was God himself coming in! Of course, Peter wouldn't have any of that! He was bursting with this commission from God – talked nineteen to the dozen before he reached our room! It had all been a spiritual experience for **him** as well. I assumed as God's sort of agent he'd come to interpret the Lord's will for us. But it was more than that. God seemed to be teaching **Peter** some new tactics as well. Apparently he'd spoken to him in a vision, telling him the Good News was for everyone – not just the Jews. That would be where I and my family came in. He was to make a special visit so that we could all be told the message.

Then we heard the whole story of Jesus and his life and death – and how God raised him up. You know it all . . . for us it was an incredible revelation. To hear it from one of Jesus' closest friends too! And to know we were **all** now included! Well, it was too much all at once. Kept thinking I was dreaming! It was what everyone longed for – a messiah offering new life to everyone, all over the world! Then as he spoke something happened – I can only liken it to one of those earth tremors where you feel the tiniest movement and everyone starts yelling! It had been silent as he was talking, then suddenly there was this racket of everyone speaking at once. In a flash I **knew** that it was the Holy Spirit! The Holy Spirit had come just for us – all of us in that room! Unthinkable, but it had happened! Peter's friends couldn't believe their eyes. Peter said we must all be baptised at once. So we were – immediately.

Can you believe it? I've known for a long time that God was with me, but now it's an open campaign! He's for everyone! What a huge advance this must have been for the Jesus followers! No stopping the troops now – the news will go all over the world!

BIBLE PASSAGES

Acts 10:1-8

There was a man in Caesarea named Cornelius, who was a captain in the Roman regiment called 'The Italian Regiment'. He was a religious man; he and his whole family worshipped God. He also did much to help the Jewish poor people and was constantly praying to God. It was about three o'clock one afternoon when he had a vision, in which he clearly saw an angel of God come in and say to him, 'Cornelius!'

He stared at the angel in fear and said, 'What is it, sir?'

The angel answered, 'God is pleased with your prayers and works of charity, and is ready to answer you. And now send some men to Joppa for a certain man whose full name is Simon Peter. He is a guest in the home of a tanner of leather named Simon, who lives by the sea.' Then the angel went away, and Cornelius called two of his house servants and a soldier, a religious man who was one of his personal attendants. He told them what had happened and sent them off to Joppa.

Acts 10:19-34

Peter was still trying to understand what the vision meant, when the Spirit said, 'Listen! Three men are here looking for you. So get ready and go down, and do not hesitate to go with them.' So Peter went down and said to the men, 'I am the man you are looking for. Why have you come?'

'Captain Cornelius sent us,' they answered. 'He is a good man who worships God and is highly respected by all the Jewish people. An angel of God told him to invite you to his house, so that he could hear what you have to say.' Peter invited the men in and persuaded them to spend the night there.

The next day he got ready and went with them; and some of the believers from Joppa went along with him. The following day he arrived in Caesarea, where Cornelius was waiting for him, together with relatives and close friends that he had invited. As Peter was about to go in, Cornelius met him, fell at his feet, and bowed down before him. But Peter made him rise. 'Stand up,' he said; 'I myself am only a man.' Peter kept on talking to Cornelius as he went into the house, where he found many people gathered. He said to them, 'You yourselves know very well that a Jew is not allowed by his religion to visit or associate with Gentiles. But God has shown me that I must not consider any person ritually unclean or defiled. And so when you sent for me, I came without any objection. I ask you, then, why did you send for me?'

Cornelius said, 'It was about this time three days ago that I was praying in my house at three o'clock in the afternoon. Suddenly a man dressed in shining clothes stood in front of me and said: "Cornelius! God has heard your prayer and has taken notice of your works of charity. Send someone to Joppa for a man whose full name is Simon Peter. He is a guest in the home of Simon the tanner of leather, who lives by the sea." And so I sent for you at once, and you have been good enough to come. Now we are all here in the presence of God, waiting to hear anything that the Lord has instructed you to say.'

Peter began to speak.

Acts 10:44-48

While Peter was still speaking, the Holy Spirit came down on all those who were listening to his message. The Jewish believers who had come from Joppa with Peter were amazed that God had poured out his gift of the Holy Spirit on the Gentiles also. For they heard them speaking in strange tongues and praising God's greatness. Peter spoke up: 'These people have received the Holy Spirit, just as we also did. Can anyone, then, stop them from being baptised with water?' So he ordered them to be baptised in the name of Jesus Christ. Then they asked him to stay with them for a few days.

Psalm 147:10-11

His pleasure is not in strong horses,
Nor his delight in brave soldiers;
But he takes pleasure in those who honour him,
In those who trust in his constant love.

ADDITIONAL BIBLE REFERENCES FOR PRIVATE STUDY

Acts 10:9-18

Acts 10:35-43
Acts 11:4-17 (the second account of the conversion of Cornelius)

Matthew 28:16-20

BACKGROUND NOTES

1. Caesarea

Caesarea is in northern Palestine, about sixty-five miles north-west of Jerusalem. Before Herod the Great's time its harbour had been shallow, and unsatisfactory due to strong southerly winds, but Herod deepened it and built a breakwater to afford protection from the wind. The site of the port had been given to him by the Emperor Augustus, and in the space of twelve years (22-10BC) he transformed it into a magnificent seaport, provincial capital and celebrated trading centre. He changed the old name (Strato's Tower) to Caesarea in honour of the emperor.

The new harbour was flanked by white shining marble walls, with statues of Roma and Augustus at the entrance. The splendid new buildings included a theatre, amphitheatre, hippodrome, colonnaded street and imposing temple. Herod brought in fresh water through a handsome arched brick aqueduct, and founded a garrison in the city to protect city, harbour and water supply.

Caesarea was a predominantly pagan city and centre of hellenism at this time, but had a substantial Jewish minority.

2. Cornelius the centurion

The Italian regiment stationed at Caesarea would be a cohort of a Roman legion (a force of six thousand men) and it would number anything from three to six hundred men. A centurion was a non-commissioned officer who had worked his way up through the ranks to take command of a group of one hundred soldiers – similar to a captain in the British army today.

We are told Cornelius was widely known as a good, devout and spiritually sensitive Roman army officer, which is interesting in a period when the Roman soldiers were not always popular. We read of other good centurions in the New Testament, and scholars suggest that the Romans may have appointed particularly diplomatic and able men to handle the difficult duties of the Palestinian area. It was a sensitive, volatile region which needed careful handling. It may be that men who found Judaism appealing were considered particularly suitable. It is easy to see why Cornelius was a good candidate to further God's mission to the Gentiles.

3. Significant spread of the Gospel

Luke describes the conversion of Cornelius twice over – first as a straight narrative of the events, and then as a report given by Peter to his believer critics back in Jerusalem. This is an indication of the importance Luke attaches to the episode. It would be notable for three reasons:

a)   It was a landmark in the spread of the Gospel from its strictly Jewish beginnings to the Gentile world, and Roman Empire in particular. Luke is careful to make us aware that a large group of people were baptised with Cornelius, not just the centurion himself.

b)   It was a turning point in Peter's understanding of God's purpose for his mission. By baptising the Gentile family Peter accepts that God wants all people to come into a relationship with Jesus Christ, whether or not they have qualified for conversion to Judaism.

c)   It was important because of the attitude of the believers back in Jerusalem. Peter's report must have been powerful, to convince them that the conversions were valid without the prior affiliation with Judaism. Peter had, of course, taken six believers with him on the trip to Caesarea, so they would have been useful witnesses. William Barclay notes that in Egyptian law, which would be familiar to the Jews, seven was the figure of witnesses needed to prove a case; and in Roman law seven seals were necessary to authenticate an important document. Perhaps this was in Peter's mind when he settled for six fellow-travellers.

DISCUSSION TOPICS

1.   Are some careers difficult to reconcile with being a practising Christian?

2.   Our society is often troubled by the undisciplined behaviour of yobs and vandals. Have you any suggestions as to how this problem might be solved?

3.   Why do we have a problem with people of other races? What initiatives can churches take to break down prejudice?

4.   Are you aware of prejudice of any sort in the life of your church?

5.   Who would you choose as a good role model for your life?

6. Do you ever invite people to come and 'hear God's message', as Cornelius did?

7. How do you react to new ideas for worship? Which do you welcome, and which do you find difficult?

PRAYER

Lord, make me an instrument of your peace:
Where there is hatred, let me sow love;
Where there is injury, pardon;
Where there is doubt, faith;
Where there is darkness, light;
Where there is despair, hope;
And where there is sadness, joy.

Divine master, grant that I may not so much seek
to be consoled as to console,
to be understood as to understand,
to be loved as to love.

For it is in giving that we receive,
It is in pardoning that we are pardoned,
And in dying that we are born to eternal life.

Francis of Assisi (1181-1226)

PETER

Hi, folks! Come on in! What a great time it is – I'm so glad you're here!
Things are really moving! Since the Spirit came, the Gospel has been
spreading like wildfire. It keeps us on the go night and day – running the
Jerusalem set-up, backing up Philip's work in Samaria, charging off to
Caesarea – you never know what the next day will bring! We're really on a
roll!

For me personally, it's a new life – simple as that! And that's exactly what
Jesus predicted, so why be surprised? A short while ago I could have
swallowed hemlock. When Jesus was crucified it was the end for me. I'd
even deserted him in his moment of need . . . you can't easily live with that,
you know. But that's all water under the bridge, and I've moved on. When
Jesus came back, he knew what I was going through. He gave me express
instructions to look after his sheep, as he called them; that meant his followers
– and he spelt it out to me three times. I realised he was carefully cancelling
out the three times I'd lied to people that I didn't know him. It was his way of
showing he still trusted me. So what could I do but pick myself up and get
moving? I threw myself into organising and encouraging the Jerusalem
believers.

Soon after that Jesus left finally, and we were all gutted. But we returned to
Jerusalem and I remember clinging to his promise that the Holy Spirit would
come to support us. Not half it did . . . a few days later! Hallelujah! What an
experience! Hopeless to try and describe it! If I tell you our quiet little
gathering suddenly turned into uproar, with everyone babbling at once, that
gives you some idea. But for me personally it was a sense of power . . . no, not
exactly . . . it was a sense of **being empowered.** I had this terrific urge to
speak out and win souls for Jesus! Words seemed to flow so easily and yet
I've never been one for making speeches. The Holy Spirit makes you ready
for anything, ready to be daring, ready to face any challenge for the Lord. It's
been that way ever since; and dear Lord! have we had some challenges!

But isn't it funny how you never stop learning? I used to go fishing with my
dad whenever I could – right from so high. By the time I was fifteen I was
competent – took the boat out with my brother and our mates, brought the
catch in, sorted it, dished it out . . . everything! I knew the lot! So that became
my living – and a good living it was! Then Jesus called us, it was a new way
of life, so we had to start all over again. Since his death things have changed
even more: in the community of believers I've had to handle everything from
petty squabbles about food to harassment by the authorities – things I didn't

even know about as a fisherman. I've even been in prison once, and I wouldn't be surprised if it happened again. We're walking a tightrope with the officials; they can see we're gaining converts every day, and they don't like it – they're out for our blood. By the way, in case you wonder how I got out of prison, an angel came and unlocked the door – cool as you please – and told us to go and teach in the Temple! Imagine the authorities! They were speechless!

But I was saying about learning new things: the most recent one is something I'd never have believed if it hadn't happened to me. What d'you think of this? After a lifetime of knowing that we Jews are special and the messiah will come for us alone, all of a sudden God puts me straight that this is not the case! The messiah – who, of course, is Jesus Christ – the messiah is for everyone, and I'm the one who must tell people! He showed me this in a vision the other day – a really vivid one, it's still there in my mind now.

A sheet thing came down from the sky, and it was sort of suspended by the corners. I suddenly realised it was full of birds and fish and animals – every creature you could think of. Then a voice boomed out, telling me to kill them and eat them. I couldn't do that! I've never touched anything unclean. So I refused! But the voice persisted: don't consider anything unclean that God has called clean, it said. All that happened three times over. That was all, but as it ended some strangers arrived at my house. I was still in a daze, but the Spirit nudged me and said this was part of God's plan for me. To cut a long story short, I had to go hotfoot to Caesarea where I ended up baptising a whole load of Gentiles! And what fine folk they were! So you can see I just never know what's round the corner! But you have this great sense of the Holy Spirit guiding and supporting you – it never occurs to me that I've got the wrong end of the stick, that I've read the message wrong – you know what I mean. Pray God it will always be like this!

Needless to say, some pretty awkward questions were asked about those baptisms, by the folk back in Jerusalem. I mean, it's not surprising! Some thought I'd lost my marbles! Normally I'd have been worried about how to convince them; let's face it, your emotions get carried away on a big occasion, but that won't wash with people analysing it in the cold light of day. Anyhow I just gave them the facts and – God be praised – they accepted it! As I said, what a great time this is!

But it's certainly cat and mouse with the authorities in Jerusalem right now – here's hoping we can keep a step ahead!

BIBLE PASSAGES

Acts 10:9-20

The next day, as they were on their way and coming near Joppa, Peter went up on the roof of the house about noon in order to pray. He became hungry and wanted something to eat; while the food was being prepared, he had a vision. He saw heaven opened and something coming down that looked like a large sheet being lowered by its four corners to the earth. In it were all kinds of animals, reptiles, and wild birds. A voice said to him, 'Get up, Peter; kill and eat!'

But Peter said, 'Certainly not, Lord! I have never eaten anything ritually unclean or defiled.'

The voice spoke to him again, 'Do not consider anything unclean that God has declared clean.' This happened three times, and then the thing was taken back up into heaven.

While Peter was wondering about the meaning of this vision, the men sent by Cornelius had learnt where Simon's house was, and they were now standing in front of the gate. They called out and asked, 'Is there a guest here by the name of Simon Peter?'

Peter was still trying to understand what the vision meant, when the Spirit said, 'Listen! Three men are here looking for you. So get ready and go down, and do not hesitate to go with them, for I have sent them.'

Acts 11:1-4 and 17-18

The apostles and the other believers throughout Judea heard that the Gentiles also had received the word of God. When Peter went to Jerusalem, those who were in favour of circumcising Gentiles criticised him, saying, 'You were a guest in the home of uncircumcised Gentiles, and you even ate with them!' So Peter gave them a complete account of what had happened from the very beginning . . .

'It is clear that God gave those Gentiles the same gift that he gave us when we believed in the Lord Jesus Christ; who was I, then, to try to stop God!'

When they heard this, they stopped their criticism and praised God, saying, 'Then God has given to the Gentiles also the opportunity to repent and live!'

'Do not eat anything that the Lord has declared unclean. You may eat these animals: cattle, sheep, goats, deer, wild sheep, wild goats, or antelopes – any animals that have divided hoofs and that also chew the cud. But no animals may be eaten unless they have divided hoofs and also chew the cud. You may not eat camels, rabbits, or rock-badgers. They must be considered unclean; they chew the cud but do not have divided hoofs. Do not eat pigs. They must be considered unclean; they have divided hoofs but do not chew the cud. Do not eat any of these animals or even touch their dead bodies.

You may eat any kind of fish that has fins and scales, but anything living in the water that does not have fins and scales may not be eaten; it must be considered unclean.

You may eat any clean bird. But these are the kinds of birds you are not to eat: eagles, owls, hawks, falcons; buzzards, vultures, crows; ostriches; seagulls, storks, herons, pelicans, cormorants; hoopoes; and bats.

All winged insects are unclean; do not eat them. You may eat any clean insect.

Do not eat any animal that dies a natural death. You may let the foreigners who live among you eat it, or you may sell it to other foreigners. But you belong to the Lord your God; you are his people.

Do not cook a young sheep or goat in its mother's milk.'

ADDITIONAL BIBLE REFERENCES FOR PRIVATE STUDY

John 21:14-19

Leviticus 11:1-47

BACKGROUND NOTES

1. Peter the fisherman

Peter was a native of Bethsaida near the Lake of Galilee, and was a hard-working independent master-fisherman in Capernaum with his brother Andrew when first mentioned in the Gospels. His native language would have been Aramaic although, since Galilee was a region surrounded by Gentiles, he was probably also familiar with colloquial Greek. When he appeared before the

Sanhedrin with John (Acts 4:13) they are described as 'ordinary men of no education'. This would mean no technical education in the intricacies of the law, and no professional qualifications.

2. Peter the Rock

Peter is the first to recognise Jesus as the Messiah (Matthew 16:15-18) when the disciples are asked who they think he is. Jesus commends Peter and calls him the rock on which God's church will be built. However, subsequent events show him to be a likeable but impetuous, inconsistent and at times weak character – hardly worthy of such a title.

The turning-points in Peter's life are the appearance of Jesus to him after the resurrection, where he is instructed to 'feed my sheep', and the coming of the Holy Spirit at Pentecost. From then on Peter shows himself to be an undoubted leader, a conscientious believer, a kindly team-mate, a courageous champion and missionary of the Early Church – a true rock in unstable and challenging times.

3. Peter the preacher

Peter's sermons in Acts are long and detailed, and it is unlikely that anyone would have remembered them verbatim throughout the thirty or so years before Luke recorded the events. So the writer either had access to another source which recorded the sermons, or he improvises with what he is confident Peter would have said. Scholars do not know which of these options is correct. However, the sermons recorded in Acts all follow a similar format, and the themes contained in them are fundamental to the preaching ascribed to the Early Church missionaries. They are as follows:

a) The age of the messiah has dawned. A new order will begin and God's elect are called to join the new community.

b) This new age has been brought about by the life, death and resurrection of Jesus Christ, which all fulfil the Old Testament prophecies, and can therefore be seen to be part of God's plan.

c) Through his resurrection Jesus is elevated to the right hand of God and is the Saviour of the new Israel.

d) Christ will return in glory and will judge the living and the dead.

e) People must therefore repent so that they may be forgiven, receive the Holy Spirit and have eternal life.

What is conspicuously missing from the early Christian preaching is advice on moral standards and the suitable duties and way of life of practising followers of Jesus.

Whether or not the sermons are an accurate representation of Peter's words, there can be no doubt that he was a charismatic, powerful and persuasive preacher, and that this gift was a characteristic of the new Peter empowered by the Holy Spirit.

4. Peter the orthodox Jew

In Jesus' time no orthodox Jew would enter the home of a Gentile – even a God-fearer such as Cornelius – nor would he himself offer hospitality to a Gentile. Rubbing shoulders with Gentiles was forbidden and orthodox Jews would not sit down at table with them. This immediately precluded Gentiles from the community of the Early Church since its pattern of life centred on the shared sacrament of the Lord's Supper. Moreover the Jewish food laws were very strict, indicating which foods were 'clean' and could be eaten, and which were 'unclean' and forbidden (see Leviticus 11).

Peter is already disobeying these rules when he lodges in the house of Simon the leather-worker, whose trade would have rendered him 'unclean'. While staying there Peter receives divine guidance in the form of a vision as he is contemplating his next meal; a display of animals and birds is used to convey to Peter not only that he must abolish distinctions between the cleanliness of different foods but, more importantly, he must abolish distinctions of human race and class. He is told that God does not show partiality to the Jews or to anybody else, and that such distinctions must no longer be made between Jews and Gentiles. The fact that the Holy Spirit comes down on Cornelius and his Gentile gathering is further proof that this is God's will. As the Gospel spreads Gentiles will be included in the body of believers.

Peter has had to move a long way from the accepted traditions of his upbringing and life hitherto.

DISCUSSION TOPICS

1. The word 'power' occurs frequently in Acts. What sort of power is it and how might we experience it in our lives?

2. Have you ever had to make a radical switch from established attitudes or beliefs of your past? What prompted this, and how did you manage?

3. Can you quote any example of what you see as God influencing the course of your life – either directly or indirectly?

4. In what ways might our faith require us to show courage in our twenty-first century society?

5. What gifts and personal characteristics can you identify in Peter? Are they different from those of Peter the fisherman in the pages of the Gospels?

6. Many people grow up in our society with practically no knowledge of the Christian faith. Should something be done about this?

PRAYER

Lord God, Giver of Life, who sweeps away the dead wood of the garden and nourishes in its place the sprouting green of springtime,

We marvel at the way you transformed the apostle Peter:
We thank you for forgiving the weakness which led him to betray you; not only did you give him a fresh start, but you entrusted to him an even greater privilege – the care of your sheep. We praise you for the power of the Holy Spirit which filled him
– with strength to lead the disciples;
– with eloquence and fluency to preach to the crowds;
– with courage to face persecution;
– with joy and enthusiasm to proclaim your message of love and salvation.

Lord God, Giver of Life,
We ask you to change us as you changed Peter.
We are sorry for the wrong things we have done, and the ways in which we have let you down. We pray for your forgiveness, and for a fresh start to serve you better.
Open our hearts to receive your Holy Spirit so that, by his power, we may be
– inspired in our witness;
– dedicated in our work for your worldwide Church;
– loving and tolerant in our relationships;
– committed to the spread of your Kingdom here on earth.

Lord God, Giver of Life, draw everything in the garden towards the warm light of your everlasting love.
We ask it for Jesus Christ's sake,

AMEN

MARY, MOTHER OF JOHN MARK

Hallo, how are you? Do come in! Rhoda told me we had some more visitors. I hope you weren't kept waiting too long outside the gate? It's so hot. But we have to be very careful, you see. I detest all the secrecy and locked doors – it's the opposite of everything I've worked for – but we know there are spies everywhere at the moment, determined to persecute the followers of the Way.

Come on in and take the weight off your feet. I'm Mary, by the way. I expect you know my son, John – or John Mark, as he seems to be called. Perhaps you've also met my relative from Cyprus, a lovely man called Barnabas? Both are up to their eyes in the Lord's work, and are for ever popping in and out of my house. You probably know this is the Jerusalem headquarters of the believers, so the house is usually bursting at the seams. And it isn't as though it's a poky widow's place – I was fortunate to be left with such a lovely spacious home, so it's ideal for the purpose; with all these rooms opening off the courtyard, I can accommodate a whole army! We did have a quiet spell when the first persecutions started a while back, and everyone went off to places like Samaria to set up missionary work there; only the apostles stayed here in Jerusalem. There was no point in the others all hanging around and getting arrested. But, of course, numbers are building up again very rapidly as new converts join us. I'll soon be out of floor space! There's never a dull moment, I can tell you!

In fact, if these walls could talk, they'd have some thrilling stories to tell. Now and again I hear the servants chattering excitedly about this or that happening in the house, and I have to remind them discretion is the order of the day – no careless gossip with their young men, or their little brothers and sisters; walls have ears, I keep telling them! They are good, trustworthy girls, though; I'm well blessed. Actually, one of them – Rhoda – was an example to us all the other day, and taught us a salutary lesson! We still have a giggle about it. It was ironical that she behaved in exactly the way I have trained her – observed my instructions to the letter – but when it came to it, no one took the poor girl seriously! I don't know how I could be so stupid! Luckily she was very determined – stuck to her guns, and everything turned out all right.

It was one of those nights of high drama which are fast becoming the norm at my house. We'd had a really bad set-back, and I suppose it had knocked us all a bit off course. One of our key people had been murdered by the authorities. It was James – one of the Sons of Thunder, as Jesus called them. It was horrendous. King Herod Agrippa suddenly launched out on a new campaign of persecution, and had him beheaded without any warning. We couldn't believe it – whatever was the point? That won't stop people from following our Lord – more likely the opposite. Anyway, the next thing that happened was, in the Festival of Unleavened Bread, Peter was arrested. Of course, we were sure the same thing would happen. We held a constant prayer vigil night and day, as we always do, but I have to admit our hearts were heavy and full of foreboding. Peter has escaped before, and we felt sure no mercy would be shown this time. Little did we know that God himself had already taken command! He had sent an angel to lead Peter out of the prison, and he was on his way here. Suddenly in the middle of the night there was knocking on our outside door – not loud, but quite persistent. Rhoda went to answer it, and she says she immediately recognised the low voice as Peter's. She knew she mustn't open the door in case it was a trick, so she rushed back excitedly to tell us. She was thrilled to bits and just couldn't understand our reaction. But I'm ashamed to say that none of us believed her; we thought she'd taken leave of her senses – imagined it was his voice. It was just wishful thinking, we concluded! But you see we were all forgetting the power of our great Lord God. Here we were, praying with all our hearts, but forgetting that our prayers could be answered! What feeble creatures we humans are!

Anyway, dear Rhoda refused to take no for an answer, and by then we could all hear the furious knocking. We went to the gate, and there he was – Peter – as large as life, and distinctly unhappy about our welcome! Oh dear me! After all he'd been through! Just imagine if the guards had caught up and spirited him away again – we'd never have forgiven ourselves. It doesn't bear thinking about. In the event, he'd decided not to stay in Jerusalem – he'd just come to tell us he was free – so, of course, we couldn't fuss over him and make amends for our mistake. He was sure King Herod's men would come looking for him at my house, so he just grabbed a bite to eat and disappeared again into the night. What a to-do! I suddenly felt very humble. If it hadn't been for my servant girl, things might have turned out very differently. I shall certainly take more notice of them in future.

So that was the last bit of excitement; the believers have been coming and going without incident since then, praise God! Long may it last! I sometimes find myself wishing we could go back to the days when friends visited freely without all this anxiety. Even at the time when Jesus invited the disciples here for his last supper party, things were more normal. He fixed it up quite secretly, but we didn't have to worry about spies and persecutions then. And, of course, more recently when the followers came to live here after Jesus went up to heaven, those were great times of fellowship. It was a new life for everyone – living, eating, praying, sharing together – but it was a time of great joy. I can't help thinking of all that when times are hard, but then I give myself a stern talking-to! What an ungrateful girl you are, Mary! To think that God has chosen your home to be the focus of his work in Jerusalem!

What greater privilege could you ask for? So I say a little prayer, give myself a shake, and hurry off to see what's what! We housewives are all the same, aren't we? When your mind gets bogged down with worry, the best thing is to roll up your sleeves and give the mats a good beating!

BIBLE PASSAGES

Acts 12:6-17

The night before Herod was going to bring him out to the people, Peter was sleeping between two guards. He was tied with two chains, and there were guards on duty at the prison gate. Suddenly an angel of the Lord stood there, and a light shone in the cell. The angel shook Peter by the shoulder, woke him up, and said, 'Hurry! Get up!' At once the chains fell off Peter's hands. Then the angel said, 'Fasten your belt and put on your sandals.' Peter did so, and the angel said, 'Put your cloak round you and come with me.' Peter followed him out of the prison, not knowing, however, if what the angel was doing was real; he thought he was seeing a vision. They passed by the first guard post and then the second, and came at last to the iron gate leading into the city. The gate opened for them by itself, and they went out. They walked down a street, and suddenly the angel left Peter.

Then Peter realised what had happened to him, and said, 'Now I know that it is really true! The Lord sent his angel to rescue me from Herod's power and from everything the Jewish people expected to happen.'

Aware of his situation, he went to the home of Mary, the mother of John Mark, where many people had gathered and were praying. Peter knocked at the outside door, and a servant named Rhoda came to answer it. She recognised Peter's voice and was so happy that she ran back in without opening the door, and announced that Peter was standing outside. 'You are mad!' they told her. But she insisted that it was true. So they answered, 'It is his angel.'

Meanwhile Peter kept on knocking. At last they opened the door, and when they saw him, they were amazed. He motioned with his hand for them to be quiet, and he explained to them how the Lord had brought him out of prison. 'Tell this to James and the rest of the believers,' he said; then he left and went somewhere else.

Acts 1:12-14

Then the apostles went back to Jerusalem from the Mount of Olives, which is about a kilometre away from the city. They entered the city and went up to the room where they were staying: Peter, John, James and Andrew, Philip and Thomas, Bartholomew and Matthew, James son of Alphaeus, Simon the Patriot, and Judas son of James. They gathered frequently to pray as a group, together with the women and with Mary the mother of Jesus and with his brothers.

ADDITIONAL BIBLE REFERENCES FOR PRIVATE STUDY

Luke 8:1-3

Acts 11:19-24

BACKGROUND NOTES

1. Mary's house

Jesus was known to have a number of wealthy women among his followers who used their resources to support his work. It was common for rabbis to be assisted in this way. Mary would have been one of these since she was certainly a widow of considerable means. Not only did she have servants, but she had a house big enough to accommodate large numbers for prayer. There are further clues to the spaciousness of her house in the reference to an outer door or vestibule on to the road, and perhaps in the mental image of the servant girl rushing back and forth which suggests some distance – possibly across a courtyard.

The fact that Peter went straight to Mary's house after escaping from prison makes it likely that this was the principal meeting place of the Jerusalem believers, especially since the message he brings is for James, their leader. Popular legends of the Early Church earmark it also as the apostles' lodging house after Christ's ascension, and the location of Jesus and the disciples' gathering for the Last Supper. The latter presents a slight problem since Gospel reports suggest a male owner (*'Then he will show you a large upstairs room . . .' Mark 14:15*), but E. M. Blaiklock suggests this might be Mary's husband who died soon after the supper meeting!

However one interprets such minor detail – especially allowing for the time which elapsed before recording took place – there is no doubt that Mary's home was an important focus for early Christian activities in Jerusalem.

2. John Mark and Barnabas

Mary is only mentioned once in the Bible, but we glean a surprising amount of information about her, including reference to two relatives. She was the mother of John Mark, whom she would certainly have addressed as John; this was his Jewish name which would have been used by family and closest friends. Mark was his Roman name which would have been used outside the home, because in occupied Palestine at that time all Jews had a Jewish and a Roman name.

The other relative mentioned is Barnabas, of whom we read more in the later chapters of Acts and in Paul's Letters. He is described as a cousin to John Mark – *'Aristarchus, who is in prison with me, sends you greetings, and so does Mark, the cousin of Barnabas' (Colossians 4:10).*

3. Herod Agrippa

This Herod is mentioned ten times in the Bible but all within Acts 12. He was the tetrarch of Galilee, and then ruler of Palestine from 41-44AD. He was a direct descendant of the Maccabees through his mother Mariamne, and no doubt for this reason was careful to curry favour with the Jews. He kept their laws and followed their observances assiduously, duly achieving popularity with them. It was probably to impress them still further that he launched into a programme of bitter persecution of the Christians. He beheaded James, the son of Zebedee – not to be confused with the James of Acts 12:17 who was the brother of Jesus and acknowledged leader of the believers at this time. Then he arrested Peter, and there is further evidence of his desire to please the orthodox Jews in that he deferred the trial till after the Passover; it was a Jewish rule that no trial or execution could take place during the week-long Festival of Unleavened Bread.

It is ironic that Herod's persecution of the Christians was prompted more by fostering support for himself than by any disagreements of principle.

DISCUSSION TOPICS

1. What importance do you attach to prayer?

2. How does worry affect you, and what do you think is the best way to handle it?

3. Are some jobs in the church more important than others? Which tend to be overlooked or taken for granted?

4. How highly do you rate a talent for hospitality?

5. What are the essential ingredients of a healthy church life?

6. Most churches have far more women than men nowadays. Has Christianity become a way of life for women rather than men?

7. What insights have the ten characters of this book given you into the nature and working of the Holy Spirit?

PRAYER

Come down, O Love divine,
Seek thou this soul of mine,
And visit it with thine own ardour glowing;
O Comforter, draw near,
Within my heart appear,
And kindle it, thy holy flame bestowing.

O let it freely burn,
Till earthly passions turn
To dust and ashes, in its heat consuming;
And let thy glorious light
Shine ever on my sight,
And clothe me round, the while my path illuming.

Let holy charity
Mine outward vesture be,
And lowliness become mine inner clothing;
True lowliness of heart,
Which takes the humbler part,
And o'er its own shortcomings weeps with loathing.

And so the yearning strong,
With which the soul will long,
Shall far outpass the power of human telling;
For none can guess its grace,
Till he become the place
Wherein the Holy Spirit makes his dwelling.

Bianco da Siena (d.1434)
tr. R. F. Littledale (1833-90)

BIBLIOGRAPHY

Good News Bible, special edition in full colour with features by Lion, the Bible Society.

David Robinson, ed., *Concordance to the Good News Bible,* British and Foreign Bible Society.

William Barclay, *The Acts of the Apostles*

William Barclay, *The Letters of James and Peter*

William Barclay, *God's Young Church*

John R. W. Stott, *The Message of Acts*

John Stott, revised Stephen Motyer, *Men with a Message*

Richard N. Longenecker, *Expositor's Bible Commentary – Acts*

Herbert Lockyer, *All the Men of the Bible*

Herbert Lockyer, *All the Women of the Bible*

Josephus, *The Jewish War*

Morna Hooker, *Studying the New Testament*

Tim Dowley, *The Student Guide to Life in Bible Times*

The Encyclopedia of the Bible, Lion

Handbook to the Bible, Lion

Packer, Tenney and White, *Marshall's Bible Handbook,* Marshall, Morgan and Scott

Black and Rowley, eds., *Peake's Commentary on the Bible,* Nelson

Jesus and his Times, Reader's Digest

E. M. Blaiklock, *Today's Handbook of Bible Characters,* Bethany House

William L. Coleman, *Today's Handbook of Bible Times and Customs,* Bethany House

Ronald Brownrigg, *Who's Who in the New Testament,* Dent

ACKNOWLEDGEMENTS

All scripture quotations are from the *Good News Bible* published by the Bible Societies/HarperCollins Publishers Ltd. U.K. copyright American Bible Society, 1966, 1971, 1976, 1992, and are used with the permission of the publishers.

Thanks, as ever, to my husband John, and daughters Liz and Kate, for correction of my work and suggestions for improvement.